Happy
Pretty
Messy

Happy Pretty Messy

CULTIVATING BEAUTY *and* BRAVERY *when* LIFE GETS TOUGH

Natalie Wise

Skyhorse Publishing

Illustrations by Emily Batchelder

"I Have Confidence" by Richard Rodgers, copyright © 1964 Williamson Music (ASCAP), an Imagem Company, owner of publication and allied rights throughout the World. International Copyright Secured. All Rights Reserved. Used by Permission.

All poetry is by Natalie Wise unless otherwise indicated and was originally published in *Darling Magazine*.

Skyhorse Publishing books may be purchased in bulk at special discounts for sales promotion, corporate gifts, fund-raising, or educational purposes. Special editions can also be created to specifications. For details, contact the Special Sales Department, Skyhorse Publishing, 307 West 36th Street, 11th Floor, New York, NY 10018 or info@skyhorsepublishing.com.

Skyhorse® and Skyhorse Publishing® are registered trademarks of Skyhorse Publishing, Inc.®, a Delaware corporation.

Visit our website at www.skyhorsepublishing.com.

10 9 8 7 6 5 4 3 2 1

Library of Congress Cataloging-in-Publication Data is available on file.

Cover design by Abigail Gehring
Cover image courtesy of iStock.com

Hardcover ISBN: 978-1-5107-0941-6
Paperback ISBN: 978-1-5107-5173-6
Ebook ISBN: 978-1-5107-0942-3

Printed in China

Dedicated to my friends and family. I say with conviction:
I choose you and I'm so glad we get to do life together.
Thank you for everything.

Contents

Introduction

Beauty and bravery. Tough words, right? But they are the foundation of a deep life and are well worth cultivating. And learned skills they are. Even if you were never taught how to live with beauty and bravery, don't fret. True, tending a life of purpose is no easy feat, and requires deep heart-work. But, oh, oh, it is worthy heart-work. A free heart is so joyful and light that it simply radiates beauty and bravery into the world. This is what we seek, to carry beauty, to be brave, to live with love and passion, and to let everyone know this: We are here. And for that, we don't apologize.

Living with beauty and bravery are often one and the same thing, and sometimes they are polar opposites. Sometimes beauty requires bravery and bravery requires beauty. Sometimes bravery and beauty each require the deep-down not-so-pretty stuff of life. But we go there—for the beauty that comes afterwards, for the beauty that is found in the soul of the human spirit, especially in suffering. We show up. We do the work. We get some dirt under our fingernails and on our hearts because that is the stuff of life, too.

I will go, I will stay, I will cry it out and breathe through it, and I will be purposely present, and I will be passionately patient, hard as it is. I've been sifting through this idea of "passionate patience" in my heart. It comes from Romans 5:3–5, in the Message translation. I am here. No more lackluster living and loving. And I'm really going to try to cool it on the anxiety thing.

I want to be beautiful and brave.

There, I said it out loud.

A builder-upper, not fixer-upper. A brave-hearted giver, lover, daughter, sister, friend. A beauty-filled beauty-finder who celebrates life because I deem it worthy of celebration. Who lives a "happy-pretty-messy" life, as I like to call it.

I want to be someone who says it out loud. Someone who speaks. Someone who gives voice to the vulnerability inside me so that others can embrace their own brave.

I want to tell you something else, too. I want to tell you this: Your life doesn't have to have a sad story. There are enough stories like that.

No one is hopeless. No one is utterly unloved. And if you feel like you are, come here. I will give you a hug, I will feed you, I will hand you coffee . . . just come.

I am a writer and I wish I could change the words of many stories we've lived. I wish the version in my head played out on the streets and we all stood amazed at the fact that sometimes there are pink clouds on a blue sky in August. But sometimes it rains for weeks on end and we lose heart.

I have been where brave was nowhere to be found, where beauty seemed a distant concept. I'm really nothing special. I'm half tummy flab and bad decisions, another half bad jokes and bad timing. But I found my way back to brave. You can, too.

✑ ✑ ✑

It's time now. Time to open our hearts. Take it all in, take it all in and move it around our hearts like salve for the weary soul. May this book be your guide to a heart wide open, a balm for your broken bravery, and a siren call of the best version of you there can possibly be: beautiful, brave, happy-pretty-messy. Sounds good to me. You in?

What is Happy, Pretty, Messy?

"Happy, Pretty, Messy" is my life motto. It signifies my philosophy for just about every area of life . . . my heart, my style, my home. It is that extra "something" that some people carry with them. It takes everything in life, all the happy pretty things and all the messy things, and puts them under one banner: brave and beautiful. It's a spring in their step, a little bit of a breeze that seems to follow them wherever they go. It's a smile, always, and gumption, moxie, and grace for themselves and others. It's my version of the French *joie de vivre*. A conviction that life is good and worth living, mess and all. It's about bravery and stepping out on life's uncertain terrain with certainty of one's self. What a beautiful thing.

It is all about adding beauty to the small things of everyday life. It is about being open but retaining the slightest bit of mystery. It's a way of being, a manner of self that offers beauty and intrigue at the same time. This is no easy trick to master, and involves a whole lot of self-confidence and assurance of one's own beauty and bravery. But once you get it, you get it: Happy, Pretty, Messy. Yes, please.

Calibrating One's Inner Self

"THINK OF ALL THE BEAUTY STILL LEFT AROUND YOU AND BE HAPPY." —ANNE FRANK

We are fragile creatures, really. Sometimes we don't even realize our hearts are broken. It is this funny thing that we can be torn apart inside-out and not realize it, not admit it to ourselves.

I have been there. I have gone down that road that leads to destruction. My boyfriend of two years died very suddenly one spring Sunday morning. It was a pulmonary embolism, a blood clot to the lungs, about ten minutes after I had seen him. We had breakfast together that morning and I sent him to his apartment across the street (we lived directly across the street from each other, isn't that cute?) to get ready for church. He never came back to get me. He never came back.

I get it. I get that it's really hard to do life with a broken heart. Sometimes nigh impossible it seems, and many deem it so. I mired in those thoughts for a while, realizing what drives people to vices, to madness, to self-destruction. Empty-hearted, quicksand grief that makes you want to spill your guts. Instead, we run until we puke, cut until we bleed, drink until we die enough ourselves. Grief is not pretty. It's pretty darn ugly and exposes the underbelly of your psyche. It hollows you out, blinds you, binds you up, and spits you back out.

Then you're supposed to do life like nothing happened. Like love is still here. Like light still looks bright. Like there are other colors than black and white and gray.

Tragedy happens to the best of us. It happens to *all* of us. It is part of life. I'm not sure we can even distinguish between the *good times* and the *bad times* because there are just *times*. There is just *life*. Just minutes and days and they are good-bad-ugly-beautiful-overwhelming. There is just life, with all its fears and failures, all its foibles and funny sense of humor, and a bit of poetic justice to keep us on our toes. A heart has to search to set itself aright just about every moment. There is an equilibrium we have to choose. A balancing point, a weight transfer where things even out and we decide to call life in all of its gutsandglory: enough. What I have is enough. This moment is enough. This place is enough. Even more than that, *I* am enough.

I won't lie, I spent the first three months in bed after Jason died. The grocery store made me feel incomprehensibly lonely. The roads were too chaotic and dangerous. People could make me quake and shiver at the slightest look. Friends came to bring me food, wash dishes, hold my hand. To sit by me as I stared silently or rambled on about details I couldn't comprehend. I gave in to the grief for a while. I don't begrudge anyone that. Grief will take you under one way or another, at one time or another, so I figure it is best to just give in when it wants to come and let it go when it wants to go. For me, that was three months of solid checking-out from life. I didn't write a word, didn't work, didn't shower except to cry at the scent of his bodywash before putting on his sweatpants again and snuggling his teddy bear to my chest. I did grief. Did ugly-cry-mourning.

And one day I noticed it was summer. It was summer. How cruel and curious a thing it was to me, to realize that the seasons had changed. But I realized it was more than simply a metaphor, it was my mid-July moment of truth. I had a bit of breath in me now. A bit of strength, as I started eating again. Junk food, but it was calories, and I had lost so much weight it wasn't hurting. I knew, deep inside but palpably, that if I continued to give in to the anxiety and grief, I would never recover. That I would die inside, and in essence two of us would have died for no reason. Instead, I wanted to live for two. How could I waste a beautiful summer afternoon in bed, not knowing if I am guaranteed another?

I changed paths. I summered, in both healthy and unhealthy ways, but I was getting it out. Processing it. I bought too many new swimsuits. Made myself go to the lake and swim every evening. Invited myself over to friends' houses for dinner. Borrowed cats and dogs and my friends' babies for snuggles. Went to the drive-in, just for me. Said yes to things I normally would have said no to, like rock climbing, rappelling, and zip lining. Went sky diving, rocky mountain climbing, 2.7 seconds on a bull named . . . no, wait, that's a song, not my life.

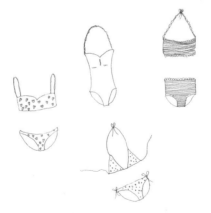

I just want to say that it *is* worth it to go through what I call the "hard heart-work" of "adulting." I know how difficult it can be. Because it is difficult many neglect it, which is a grave mistake. When we don't deal with tragedy in our lives it truly kills a part of us. If it doesn't flat-out kill us, we become so deeply hurt that we build walls and gates and put up barbed wires. It's just what we tend to do, this twisted self-protective thing that only ends up hurting us. Did you know when you put barbed wire around your heart, the barbs cut into your own heart just as deeply as they cut into others, if not more?

Hearts take a while to catch up to tragedy. Remember that. Shock is real, and the stages of grief are real. We go through the stages of grief in big and small ways for many things in life. For loss of friendship, church, community, family relationships, jobs, commitments, and the list goes on. And we have to get back to brave each time. Or slowly, over time, the little stones in our paths become giant stumbling blocks, and eventually, boulders blocking us in entirely.

• • • • • • • • • • • • • •

When I was a little girl, I saw the beauty of this, darlings:
I saw the call of the world being answered
By women with crowns on their heads and
Hearts on their sleeves, held on with superglue
So I took notes and bought myself a tube of this magic glue

These women taught me that when the road turns sharp and jars me
To bear up under courage, and find the signpost
For "Normal" and turn on my heels
To head the opposite direction
The way no one has dared travel yet
And say, "This is what I shall do today"

I head out into the world with pockets full
Of gold stars to mark the trees for the way

I will line the paths neatly with birch limbs
So others may follow in my footsteps
And find the journey slightly less arduous
For the knowledge that a friend with sure steps
Has walked this path before, too

I will dust my hands off and head toward town
For this sleepy village needs me to keep watch
While it rests, so I write words in a journal and plan
How tomorrow, I will stand under the sign that says
"Average" and I will turn on my heels and
Head towards "Astonishing"

As the dawn rolls in, I can put my feet up for a moment
And sigh
"I have spent all of my energy and I have done
A great many things and now, I do believe, I should
like some tea and perhaps a cookie."

• • • • • • • • • • • • • •

Dealing with Trauma/Hurt

There's this thing about "pulling yourself up by your own bootstraps." First off, I'm not sure what bootstraps are or how to use them to pull myself up. Instead, the image I keep in my head is those coffee-can stilts we used to make when we were kids, you know? Punch two holes on the side of each coffee can and string twine through that is long enough to make "handles." And you have to manage this tricky pulling up and moving as one with the cans and the string and then do it all over again with the other foot. Now that I've got that off my chest, we can talk about this curious phrase in a little more detail: To pull yourself up by your bootstraps.

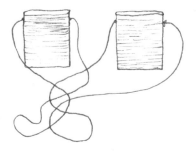

I guess it means grabbing hold of our "handles" and working on that still-tricky thing of pulling up and moving forward at the same time, one foot in front of the other. My mom always talks about handles in life and how important it is to get handles on tough situations. What is this metaphorical life-handle, other than a way of tricking our mind into finding ways to carry things that are otherwise awkward and heavy? It's a good image. My boyfriend died. Your husband left. Your kids are going crazy. How do you develop handles to help us carry those things? I think it comes down to a few things.

When Jason died I cried out to God for help during many, many sleepless nights. One night, I heard whispered into the dark room, clear and calm, "This is not meant to destroy you." Those words changed things for me. I could tuck them in my heart. This terrible thing happened. It changed my life. It's okay that I'm grieving. But I am still alive. I am still here. While this is part of my story, it is not meant to destroy me. Your story, whatever it may be, is not meant to destroy you. Grab those bootstraps, those strings-attached-to-coffee-cans, and let's work through it.

1) **Admitting it happened or is happening.** Denial is a hard-to-shake stage of grief. Being honest with ourselves is a difficult process. Grapple with it. Sit with the silence and the loneliness. You may need to talk to a dear friend or counselor to get here. *This is okay too.* You are being strong by getting help, by admitting to yourself the reality of the situation. I am so proud of you.

2) **Admitting it is affecting us.** Life is tough. It affects us because we are human. We are designed to be affected, or we would be robots.

3) **Admitting it is okay that it is affecting us.** Your life is changing or has changed somehow, quite possibly in a way you never imagined. That is hard to accept. Society gives us this misguided idea that if we just keep our head down and our schedule busy, and answer "How are you?" with "Fine," we're being strong. That is not true. Life change **changes us.** And that is okay. That is good.

4) **Boiling it down to what truly matters in the situation**. Find the linchpin in the situation. What matters most? Your children? Your own safety? Keeping family relations intact? The details are surface dust. Get rid of the dust and see what lies below. Hold on to those things.

5) **Rolling that into a little mantra of sorts to carry with us.** "Back to brave," "Zen it out," "Family first," "Embrace change," or whatever works for you. This is the thing you repeat under your breath

to yourself as you drive to a difficult meeting. That
you repeat to yourself while holding the hand of
a loved one in the hospital. Write it on your heart,
carry it with you.

back

to

brave

6) **Combining that with a good old-fashioned
bag of tricks to keep us going.** Finally, a good old-fashioned "bag
of tricks" can keep us steady when we're off-kilter in every other
area of life. The basics come first: eat well, get enough sleep, and do
gentle exercise. From there, it's all little tricks. Here are some of my
favorites:

Xylitol mints: I used to be addicted to Altoids' strong peppermint oil
that cleared my headaches, calmed my stomach, and refocused my
brain. But my dentist was not thrilled because Altoids are made with
real sugar and I was popping them like . . . well, candy. She turned
me on to these Xylitol mints I can use whenever I need a mental or
physical boost that are actually healthy for my teeth. Say what? Buy
stock now, just saying.

Elderberry zinc lozenges: When I'm feeling run-down I tend to catch
any cold going around. These elderberry zinc lozenges are a one-
two punch, and they taste good, too.

Heating pad/hot water bottle: This calming and comforting old-fashioned
remedy is like giving yourself a hug. Snuggle it up.

Keep your food simple and easy: In fact, I tend to eat the same things that
I know fuel me well and settle easily when I'm upset. I keep a stash
of good protein bars in my purse. I drink green juice like it's going
out of style (it probably will soon, but no matter).

The other basics: fluffy socks, a stuffed animal, bright pink-frosted animal crackers . . . basically embrace your inner sick child. I mean it.

There is no scale for grief. It weighs what it weighs, and you carry it on your shoulders the way you carry it. The only way to eventually set it down is to get acquainted with it for a while and feel its weight. Become aware of your body, your emotions, and your spirit. Really take stock of what you're feeling. Let it be uncomfortable. Let it hurt. The carrying is where the growth happens, and the setting down is where the freedom comes. Freedom is our ultimate goal, yes? Freedom from the pain, the past, and the pseudo-self we hide under when we're hurt.

When I want to run back to bed because I'm sad, here's what I do: admit I'm sad. Ha, just kidding, that's step 5. First, I . . .

1) Cry it out
2) Eat a cupcake/donut/three bowls of cereal/ice cream/cookie dough
3) Drink coffee at midnight
4) Throw a grown-up temper tantrum, which involves texting everyone I can think of about how upset I am, then texting them how sorry I am for texting so many times

Then I admit I'm sad. But I think we get better at recognizing it every time we do it, and can eventually shave off a few of these bad decisions. We get more comfortable admitting our emotions. I'm not sure why it can be such a big deal to admit we're sad, lonely, hurt. This is how we do life, happy-sad-lonely-full-empty-hurting-high; it's always one or more. There is no need to feel bad about this. In fact, I've found that when I admit I'm sad, it opens the door for others to speak up about their own sadness.

Loneliness is often a big part of sadness, but thankfully that's fixable. Loneliness is often self-imposed. It is my own tendency to isolate when I'm sad, and it is really the opposite of what I should do. But a body seems to resist this social medicine, and my bed calls to me stronger than anything else. Signing up for classes that I am paying for and enjoy helps me through times like this. The camaraderie builds and I find myself grabbing appetizers after improv comedy class or having a summer porch tea after meeting at a networking event.

I have no qualms texting friends, "Can I come over so I don't take a nap?" or "Do you want me for dinner tonight?" They almost always oblige. Of course, I bring coffee so I am a welcome visitor. Then I snuggle their cats/dogs/children (and let's be honest, usually drink a glass of port or wine with them after the kids go to bed) and go home feeling much better. I've been "family-d." If you have your own family, call another family and see if they want to combine forces for the evening. Chances are everyone will be up for grabbing or making a few pizzas and letting the kids play while the grown-ups get a bit of adult conversation. This feeds the soul and isn't selfish. Parents need time away, too. As adults, we have to be the guards of our own well-being.

There can be so much day left at the end of the day, you know? I'm not sure why, but it seems to be a fact of life that things seem more difficult after dark. I always cut myself a little slack when the sun sets. Turn down the lights and stretch gently. Put in your headphones and just sit in your favorite chair with your eyes closed. Try to relax every muscle in your face, and move down

your body until your stress melts away. A heating
pad or hot water bottle is a welcome friend for
this exercise, especially during the winter months.
Placed on the chest or stomach, it is very soothing. I prefer the weight of a hot water bottle to
a heating pad, but finding the right one can be
tricky. I like the soft, gently-ridged bottles, not the
stiff, chalky ones common in most pharmacies. A heart-

shaped hot water bottle is extra wonderful. These are generally kept by the
orthopedic supports (inspiring, I know). A handmade rice pouch works well,
too, microwaved to a comfortable temperature. The addition of heat along
with the weight that mimics an embrace can bring restorative power to a few
moments sinking into yourself.

If you find yourself weary from the day and unable to stay awake to
enjoy time to work on your own creative projects or time with your family or
partner, try making hot chocolate or half-caffeine coffee after work or dinner.
The low-level caffeine can keep you awake until a decent bedtime and add life
to your evenings, especially during dark winter nights. Then, about an hour
before bed, I like to take a cold or hot cup of Natural Calm. It's a magnesium
supplement that helps anxiety and sleeplessness. You can find this at your
local natural food store. Tell them I sent you. They probably won't care but it
will make me feel good about myself. Kidding.

It helps to get ready for bed before I'm zombie-tired. Brush my teeth,
wash my face, put on my pajamas . . . these simple tasks can feel overwhelming when I'm about to fall over. Don't even begin to think about putting new
sheets on the bed at 11:30 at night. I feel like a failure at life when I don't have
the energy to deal with an elasticized piece of fabric. This is easily solved with
a little planning. I get ready for bed about an hour early, and often tidy the
bathroom for the next morning. Then I get cozy and read the magazines that
pile up, the latest library book that came in on hold, or do a bit of writing
before I'm tired enough for sleep. This allows my brain to catch up with my

body and get the "tired, going to bed now!" signal that brushing my teeth and slipping into pajamas send it.

Fluidity of Identity/Back to Basics

My mom always tells me, "Go back to the basics, Natalie," whenever I'm feeling hurt, distracted, or unsure about myself and my future. Sometimes, we can't even remember what our basics are. We become disillusioned with life, work, disappointments, and stress, and we can't even remember what makes us feel alive.

Our basic foundation of everything we do should be this: We are loved, and can love in return.

When we go back to these very basics of existence, our hearts are set right again. Everything unimportant fades out of our perspectives and we are able to focus on the truth in our lives. We are loved unconditionally. No amount of heartache, pressure, failure, or lost sense of purpose can undermine that. It never changes. Secondly, we are created for a purpose. We aren't created to be the best baker of the preschool moms so we can feel good about our parenting skills. Nor the best lawyer in the courtroom so we can show everyone who told us we'd never be successful. We were created to live in freedom; otherwise, our purposes are pointless.

I know how easy it is to focus on our own desires. I like to be the best. It feels good to be well-loved by colleagues and admired by strangers. But it is empty praise without a purposeful heart.

Still, our hearts long to do something worthwhile. We wish to contribute. How do we find and define our purpose?

What is your passion? What makes your heart stir and feel alive? God created me with a passion for writing, baking, and dancing. But sometimes life is too busy for baking or dancing. Writing doesn't come easily. I get distracted. I decide for a minute that I want to be a rock star or a hardcore hiker, not a writer and baker. But I never feel fulfilled chasing after gilded worldly dreams

IT
IS
OK

instead of listening to the voice inside me that says, "There is something more here for you." Something deeper.

What unique experiences have shaped and formed your years?

What have you loved since you were a child?

What makes you get out of bed in the morning?

What makes you smile even before you've had coffee?

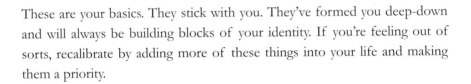

These are your basics. They stick with you. They've formed you deep-down and will always be building blocks of your identity. If you're feeling out of sorts, recalibrate by adding more of these things into your life and making them a priority.

Yes, No, and Follow-Through

Calibrating one's inner self means saying yes and no with conviction. For some of the smallest words in our language, they have some of the most

complicated meanings to us, don't they? Our hearts get tangled up in our throats when we try to say yes or no. Yes and no are a reflection of our self-worth. Some of us say yes too quickly, some say no too quickly. Both can be balanced when we use our yes and no with conviction. What do I mean by that? I mean being able to discern where the event in question fits into your life quickly and to assert that position with your response. Does this suit you? Does it excite you? Does it feel right in your gut? Is it one of your prioritized values? Does it serve someone you love and you're willing to do it with joy?

In offices they use the "deal with it once" philosophy for paperwork, and the same idea can work here, with a "respond once" philosophy. When you trust your gut and stand up for yourself, you'll be able to say no to tricky or sticky situations the first time, and right away. You will be able to say yes to worthwhile events and projects with your full commitment. It is emotionally draining to have to hem and haw and fret. Of course, some big things will require a consultation with a partner or a good "sleeping on," but otherwise, respond once.

Once you've gained confidence in your yes and no, it is time to exercise your follow-through muscles. I don't mean your muscle-through muscles, but this process may work those, too. This is follow-through on your yes or no. No one likes an unreliable, wishy-washy friend. It can be scary to be counted on. But it's the only way to grow. Stick with your decision instead of changing it, whether yes or no, unless absolutely necessary. I know how hard this can be. I'm a starter and not a finisher when it comes to projects, ideas, and events. Follow-through is a muscle I have to consistently engage to keep strong. Finishing things is good for the soul. As silly as it is, I always get a sense of accomplishment from finishing the smallest things, like a bottle of shampoo or the last slice of cheese. It is magnified when it comes to ticking off grown-up things from the to-do list, especially if they involve making phone calls to insurance or any sort of medical appointment. Reward yourself. We may be adults but we still work well with the reward system and the old-fashioned carrot-on-a-stick.

Ideas for Rewards (yay you!)

- gold stars
- smiley face stickers
- new makeup
- a new book or magazine
- a stroll through Target's dollar section
- a guilt-free fancy coffee drink
- gluten free donuts (this is seriously exciting for me)

Dreaming Again

Once you've voiced your yes and no and flexed your follow-through, it's time to start dreaming again. Oh darling, dream again. One is never too old to have a new dream. These aren't goals. These aren't necessarily even accomplishable. But a heart that is aching needs a new dream, and we must gently make room to spread our wings.

The first step towards dreaming again is knowing that it is safe. It is safe to begin dreaming again. I give you permission and a big hug, so get started. Sometimes it can be hard to dream, to think of anything to look forward to that might make you happy. Chocolate is your place to start in that case. Dream about every kind of delicious chocolate you can imagine. Then you might start thinking about the movie *Chocolat* and falling in love, or moving to France. Yes, this is all good. Or think about hot chocolate which brings you to skiing, and the Swiss Alps, and being the cutest snow bunny there ever was. Maybe chocolate makes you think of its companion, wine, which makes you think of warm California vineyards and you begin to dream of putting your feet in the Pacific Ocean with a glass of wine in your hands.

Then, dream bigger. Dream deeper. Dream with a heart wide open to possibility and savor the ideas, roll them around in your head, and relish the fantasy. This may take a great deal of time. But some day, one will stick in your heart. You'll return to it time and time again. You'll flesh it out in your mind, every little detail, dream about it day and night, doodle about it, maybe even dare to say it out loud. This is such good work, such good work.

Chances are, your basics will coincide with your dream (I love how that works!), but sometimes we are led in a new direction. Either is fine. This dream you've landed on is beautiful and precious. I'm excited for you just thinking about it, truly. Your life is about to change if you bring your whole heart to it. And that is the key.

Whole-hearted goals are directed by your heart and your intuition rather than any other influence. These goals excite you, inspire you, and push you. They require you to bring every bit of yourself to the table and to be present along the way. This is an astonishing way to operate.

Whole-hearted goals:
1) Start with your heart and have a "why"
2) Challenge you
3) Change something (there is a measure of success)

4) Bring you closer to your dream
5) Feed you instead of drain you

A whole-hearted goal gets at the why instead of just what and how. It makes you present for the process, which affects the outcome. Can you imagine if everyone were setting and achieving whole-hearted goals? Oh, that's the world I want to live in. I will make it my world, my way of living.

Cultivating Purpose

"I SAID TO MYSELF——I'LL PAINT WHAT I SEE——WHAT THE FLOWER IS TO ME BUT I'LL PAINT IT BIG AND THEY WILL BE SURPRISED INTO TAKING TIME TO LOOK AT IT——I WILL MAKE EVEN BUSY NEW YORKERS TAKE TIME TO SEE WHAT I SEE OF FLOWERS." ——GEORGIA O'KEEFE

We are brave people. We stand up for injustice and we lay down our pride and we dive head first into this big bold world so we can swim in the deep end to see what it feels like to be free in the ocean of possibility. But sometimes there seems to be too much possibility. The world seems a bit too big, with a bit too much horizon. Ironically, that can feel stifling.

I think we should go back to simple, and happy. None of this complicated hiding we do in modern life. There is no real purpose to be found there.

We say a lot of things without actually saying them. We say them with the things and people we choose to keep in our lives and say yes to, the things we  choose to say no to. We say them in roundabout ways, often circling the issue at arm's length until we get dizzy.

So let's speak up. Let's say what we mean, with purpose.

Creating a mission statement for your life lets you focus your lens on the world. It can still be wide angle, or fish eye, or macro; regardless, it will be focused on a central theme or point.

What gets you up in the morning? What makes you smile before you've had your coffee? What reassures you that today will be a good day? I know sometimes in life these questions can be hard to answer. Other times they are easy. Sometimes they are easy on the surface (kids! work!) but tough on the inside, when it comes down to your *why*.

Crafting a mission statement can begin with answering these three vital questions:

5) What is it you want to **show** the world?
6) What is it you want to **find** in the world?
7) What is the **first thing** you think about in the morning and the last thing you think about at night? This is your why. Your *because*.

The answers to these questions will be the foundation for your mission statement. Fill in the blanks: I want to show the world _____. Along the way, I am sure I will find _____. I will do these things because _____.

See, we are not called to live easy lives. We are called to live lives of love. And love is often, if not always, hard. But it is a choice.

Most of us generally know deep inside what a situation calls for, but we often bury it under external things: a sense of duty, peer pressure, a long history of wanting to please, and simple exhaustion and overwhelmption (totally a word, don't worry about it). Get out your self-reflection glass-es and your shovel and get back to your center. This is the core: Enough. I am enough. I don't need to give in to peer pressure to seem better to others. I am enough, and what I have is enough. I don't need to prove myself to others for their approval. I am enough, and while I do things out of love and choice, an overpowering sense of duty is soul-sucking. I am enough, and that means I can choose to say no as an act of self-care. I am worth these things.

I do not believe in busyness, but I do believe in purpose. I do not believe in perfection, but I do believe in purpose.

• • • • • • • • • • • • • •

I am still learning

About this thing we call life and how it works

And how we keep time here on this earth

How do we mark heaven here below

And find its mercy in our melancholy?

How do we bring it down to our hearts

And keep it there the whole year through

I do not know, do you?

How do we keep memories from slipping out to sea

And people from sailing off to destiny?

How do we tell who can hold us without hurting

Who can love us without leaving

I do not know, do you?

How do we keep pace with change, outrun fear

And never forget why we are here?

How do we fan the flames of the future

And stoke the fires of yesterday

I do not know, do you?

I am still learning

About this thing we call life and how it works

And how we keep time here on this earth

But as the year turns over and brings us a new one

I am quite certain indeed that I shall stay,

And learn, and know, and teach.

• • • • • • • • • • • • • •

Building Sustainable Lives

I talk about building a sustainable life all the time. What does it mean, exactly? Well, really, it means a solid foundation. It means putting your energy where your mind is, and doing the hard heart-work that makes a life worth living. Devotion, mission, purpose, and passion are not necessarily everyday words in this world of ours. But committing yourself to them will make your life sustainable.

Devotion: Devotion is a word that is uncool in our society right now. It smacks in the face of our too-chill-to-care culture. But it's what makes the world go 'round. It's what makes families work and businesses succeed and it is what can change one's life. Devotion elevates a task out of the realm of "duty" and brings it to the higher plane of "privilege." It is our privilege to devote ourselves to creating beautiful and sustainable lives. It is not something we must do (though we must), but something we are blessed with the ability to give ourselves to. How good it feels to have something to give yourself to. We are hearts built to spill over and into the things and people we've devoted ourselves to. Devotion is of the heart. And it's beautiful.

Passion: Passion is what makes devotion light up. While devotion is a step up from duty, passion makes devotion sustainable and exciting. Passion never quits learning, never gives up, never stops being creative, and most of all, passion never says never (even though I just did several times). Passion is what our imaginations bring to the game. Passion is what makes artists create art, what compels dancers to dance, what makes our cells come alive with excitement when we look through a microscope.

Mission: Mission is direction. It is a blueprint, a map, a goal post, and a chart that you fill in with smiley faces. Mission shows you where to go. Mission is the practical part of building a sustainable life, because without it, we'd all be passionate paupers. I'm not talking about money. Without mission, we are missing part of the equation, making us poor in persistence. With mission to show us where to go, purpose buys the plane ticket and packs the bags.

Purpose: Purpose gets you there. A mission can be laid out and planned but without a purpose, we are easily sidetracked. Purpose knows we have an end game, and that our end game is worthwhile. Purpose picks up the slack when mission gets tired. Purpose shines a light on the tough patches, gives a hand on the rocky surfaces.

All of these things come from within. All of these things are unique to you. They're you-nique (couldn't help it, sorry). A healthy heart can bring so much beauty to the world.

Let's put it together, then.
What are you devoted to?
What brings you passion?
What is your mission?
What gives your mission purpose?

Finding Your Own Voice

It can be hard to define "voice" in the metaphorical sense. We understand that everyone has a different literal voice; we sound different and it's astonishing and brilliant. We live our lives differently. We portray different things to the world, bring different things with us when we walk into a room. Even if we don't say any words, we are projecting our voice. It comes out through our style, our way of carrying ourselves, how heavy or light we step, what we hold in our hearts, and how we spend our time.

How do you find your voice? There is power in knowing what you like. Don't be a cliché unless you are one. If you don't like roses, don't say they are your favorite flower. It is perfectly acceptable to say that fuchsias are your favorites, like they are mine, or pinks or ranunculus or simple daisies or baby's breath or ferns. For Pete's sake, your favorite should be *your* favorite. I'm generally not a curve-follower. I don't like latest-craze books, or best-loved television shows when they're popular. I don't like being part of the crowd for the simple reason that I don't feel the need to be told what I should like. The best way to discover what you like is to discover. Discovering takes time and it takes a bit of effort. It takes knowing yourself, and not being afraid to admit you like something that may not be "cool."

Then again, I'm not one to like something just because it is different or unknown, either. Quirks are the stuff of life. I will forever find beauty in the gleam of whipped buttercream frosting, the way flour coats a pan, the way bread dough feels when you punch it down, and for these things I make no excuse. My best friend can't get over spreadsheets. Spreadsheets. They make her light up with organizational glee. This isn't me, but I admire the heart that she pours into it, the life she shows when she allows herself to be delighted with something simple.

My poetry professor told me a secret about poetry: You don't want to write clichés, but if you aren't toeing the line, what you're writing might not be real enough. We are all, in some way, toeing the line, because we are real. I don't like being a costumed character. I am breathing and alive, my own person who has never seen this life before, never seen this day.

But clichés are clichés for a reason: they ring true. And if your truest-you just so happens to be a cliché, girl, go big or go home. I joined a gym on New Year's Eve, so I'm with you.

Making Decisions

I'm not sure why but it seems like the biggest things in life are the hardest. Yes, the happiest are the smallest, I think, but the biggest . . . they're often difficult. Making decisions is a lifelong lesson in trusting oneself and accepting the fact that the future is unknown. Something they tell you about writing is that until a character makes a decision they have nothing. The same is true with us . . . until we make a decision we have neither option.

A decision is simply an allocation of resources, be it your time, money, energy, love, home, or anything else. So we dole out our resources with the best of intentions and with a whole heart. Put your resources where your heart is, and you've just made a good decision. My friend tells her little ones that they need "good food to make good decisions," and the same is true for adults. Good fuel for your body and brain helps us make good decisions.

When we allocate our resources through making a decision, we are saying no to something else. This is good. There are simply not enough resources to say yes to everything in any capacity. Try not to focus on what you are saying no to, and focus on the excitement of saying yes with a fullness of spirit.

We have to change our perspective a bit on how we "measure" our choices. We tend to mark decisions as good or bad based on the outcome. But that is unpredictable, and if we knew the outcome ahead of time, we wouldn't make poor choices. Measuring a choice based on the factors you put into making it is a much more reliable indicator. You can make the most solid decision on paper and in your heart and it still has an unintended consequence. This is life. Basing decisions on good intentions, your values, and your whole heart will allow you to choose with conviction, regardless of the outcome. Of course we all make choices sometimes that end in negative consequences. Then we pivot.

Transition Points and Pivoting

Pivoting is a pivotal life skill (see what I did there?). Transitions take work and a strong sense of self that we must constantly be cultivating. We have to stay in our center while pivoting to another life change. Transition points are one of our most vulnerable times, where we will need to bring all of our bravery to the table. Many of the suggestions in the "Adventuring" chapter (page 109) will be useful here, too, such as limiting decisions and changing your inner monologue. Life happens and we react. We pivot or we sit on the bench.

When we pivot, we must pull up and in at our core. That's a ballet term, to pull your tummy in and up, realigning it properly. My ballet teacher used to walk around and if you were not pulling in and up, she'd poke your tummy and say, "I can see that cheeseburger you ate for dinner." While this is not the most tactful or suggested approach, it is true. When we're not pulling in and up in our core, our less-than-savory bits show. Pulling in your core in life means doubling down on your devotion and keeping your mission front and center. Bringing discipline to the center of your being. Realigning your priorities if necessary so that the main thing remains the main thing.

Transition points are where we can very easily lose our balance. Pivoting requires taking one foot off the ground for a minute. When we're doing turns across the floor in ballet, we always have a focal point that we whip our heads around to visually "spot" with each turn. Purpose is our focus point to keep our balance. Purpose keeps you centered even when one foot is off the ground, and it keeps you going in a straight line even when you're dizzy from turning. Keep "spotting" your focal point, over and over and over again. Before you know it, you're across the room.

Sometimes our pivots are big ones that actually do require a changing of our values and mission statement. This is even harder to process and may require a mourning period. But the points remain the same: Be strong in your core, keep your focus fixed, and do the hard work.

Finding Passion Again

Sometimes in transition periods, or stagnant periods, our passion goes missing. That's okay. I am a poet, and sometimes I am living the poetry and other times I am writing the poetry. The gathering of what I call "creative capital," or the makings of passion and poetry, is a separate part of life

than the giving back of it. When we are in balance we can do this at the same time, but it's
pretty rare for the filling of the well to equal
the emptying of it creatively. Don't worry if
you go through a period of filling your well.
You will feel passion again.

Adventuring is good for this. Caffeine is
good for this. Exercising a different part of your brain is good for this (such
as taking music lessons or studying architecture). Watching old movies is good
for this. Hike a mountain. Watch a sunset. Play with kids and puppies. Make
new friends. Take an African dance class. The images, words, and little snip-
pets of life that you're taking in are creative capital.

Passion does have a price: Life. We must be living life for passion to exist. Staying within one's safety zone is a death sentence for passion. Passion
exists well outside the lines. Passion isn't patient and it won't wait forever, so
go get some. Go find it at the bottom of the Grand Canyon or at the Indiana State Corn Maze Festival. (Is that a thing? Corn mazes terrify me, please
don't invite me.)

Sometimes you have to call your own bluff to get yourself out of the
safety zone. As a writer with deadlines, I make it my number one work priority to never get writer's block. Writers are well known for washing dishes
and cleaning behind the refrigerator to avoid a blank page. I call my own
bluff often. In writer world that means filling the page with words, even
if it is mumbo jumbo and all of the Latin I remember from high school
mixed with bad poetry and movie quotes. Fill the page. Do not let your
head see a blank page. Or a blank canvas. Or an empty stage. Or a blank
equation. "Something" is something you can work with, even if artistically
it's nothing valuable. It is much easier to start from something than it is
from nothing.

With Great Love

"DO SMALL THINGS WITH GREAT LOVE" —MOTHER TERESA

Truth is, very few of us are going to be in the spotlight. And that's good. That's the way it should be. Being in the spotlight is an awful lot of pressure, and I never was much good at balancing on a pedestal. We can do things that are just as valuable without any sort of platform. Being on, or building, a platform takes time and resources from all areas of your life.

Here's a little tidbit you might not have been told: We can create actual change. Hands-on, see-it-with-our-own-eyes change. And we can see that change create more change. Being on a platform gives you fuzzy vision and a lot of words. Being on the ground gives you muddy hands and a hearty slap on the back for good work. Invest here. Invest where you are. Do simple things with every bit of passion and purpose you have. Change one life because that one life is worth changing and it matters. It matters.

You may think your passion doesn't change the world. I wrote an essay in high school about how I was going to change the world with my bakery, and I was serious. I view painting elderly people's houses as world-changing. I see planting flowers in your front yard so the neighborhood looks pretty as world-changing. I view cleaning after everyone else has gone home world-changing. I view taking kids on nature walks and teaching them poetry and teaching them basketball and listening to bird songs with them as world-changing. You, being you, offering that with grace and goodness, changes the world. Go out there, and create value for yourself and others.

We live in a culture of me first, me only mentality. An air of entitlement permeates our society. I'm not sure where we got these ideas, and I'm pretty sure they aren't good ones. Me first smacks the face of society as a whole and the greater good. Me first is a taking mentality, not a giving one. I will be a you first giver. What can I give now? What can I do immediately to make this situation better? How can I be the first to help? The best part is, when you give, this little blessing thing happens and multiplies your own blessings and life gets more beautiful. Promise.

I know they say you can't fight City Hall. I've been told that my whole life. I wanted to be an environmental activist when I was in high school. But I am not here to *fight* City Hall. City Hall, rock on with your bad self, but let's get constructive about things. Let's work together and build.

You know about guerilla gardeners, right? It's the coolest thing. They create "seed bombs" of dirt and seeds and throw them into the un-lovely areas of towns and cities to create pop-up gardens. Yes, yes. That's purpose and mission and devotion, and heck yes, that's passion.

Road-Less-Traveled Girl

I want to be the road-less-traveled girl. Do you? I will be the one who stands up for what I believe in, who is true to herself, who shows the world what she is with no reservations. I will be the one who hacks a path through the wilderness of unkindness that we have somehow cultivated. Come with me. Purpose allows us to go boldly where others dare not go. We have no fear because what we are doing is done with a whole heart and devotion to the mission. Add in a dash of passion and we're unstoppable. This is a glorious way to live. Make your own path and bring others with you. Create the world you want to live in and invite them in. Each day, each minute, actually, we are given the opportunity to choose the road less traveled. That is where I will leave my footprints.

It's easy to talk a big game, but to walk this road in reality is a bit more treacherous. I love me some high heels, I really do. But this requires my hiking boots, ya'll. And my helmet and my big-ole backpack of gear. This requires my mental machete, all of my strength of heart, and every bit of self discipline I own to keep going. I will keep going.

What is your road less traveled? Is it the road to the White House? The road to the bee hives in the back acreage? Maybe it's the road to a medical mission in the hills of India, or maybe it's the very road you live on, where hungry children cry at night. These are not the paths of least resistance. These are the paths of the most valuable results, for your inner self and for those who get to cross your path.

This life is rather simple, really. Do your best. Go where you need to go, do what needs to be done, go with your whole heart, and do it with all of the love you have and then some. And it comes back to you, it does.

Home Arts

"IT IS DELIGHTFUL WHEN YOUR IMAGINATIONS COME TRUE, ISN'T IT?" —L.M. MONTGOMERY

H ome. Oh, four letters for such a very big part of our hearts that lives outside of us. I truly believe that your surroundings affect and reflect your heart.

I've always loved the arts of homekeeping. They get lost these days amidst our busy lives. Even though we have robots that can clean our floors while we sleep and gourmet meals delivered to our doors via drone, these animatronics don't get any satisfaction from the task. Humans . . . well, we can find pleasure in the pace of keeping home. The repetitive, comforting action of homekeeping tasks is good for the brain. It opens up the creative half for daydreaming. Oh daydreaming, the stuff of poetry! A day of puttering around the home—I love to call it puttering—is good stuff, and my favorite.

Now, let me tell you a really true truth: A perfectly clean house makes me feel lonely. It seems to be waiting for a party that never arrives. Seems to echo "Alone!" to me. My whole life I've tended to fall into the messy camp. Or at least the "happy pretty messy" camp. Projects! Projects everywhere! Life in progress, here! No sadness allowed. But the older I get, the more I want the bones of my home simple. Simple and clean in the background, so the projects of my life are the decorations.

33

There are some conversations that can only be had by candlelight

Amongst the scattered dishes of four courses

Conversations that need to be aged

Like fine wine, or cheese, pressed

Between the courses of tomato caprese

And a cup of tea, or three

Conversations that remind the palate

Of clover honey and English mint with hints of sea air

And the taste of young love

When I serve beef stew, I ladle an extra

Helping of courage in case anyone is lacking

And needs to find it here, at my table

I give it generously, as well as grace and sympathy

I knead dough with a gentle hand and a quiet prayer

That these biscuits will taste good enough

To erase the abrasive moments of your day

Or maybe even your week

If blackberry jam makes you weak in the knees

Gather round the table, my darlings

Let us eat until we are full

Let us share words until we are empty of stories

And then, and only then, shall we

Slice into this heavenly tart on the sideboard

For I have gathered these plums

By golden sunlight and they have poetry to tell us

I will not need coffee in the morning, no

Instead give me the elixir of life

This drink of leftover stardust and companionship

Of a table with friends, percolating around the cookstove

Served with apples coddled in cinnamon sauce

Muffins nestled in a basket, crowned with sugar

And contentment, the choice fruit of the orchard.

The Kitchen

The kitchen really is the center of the home, as philosophers and home keepers alike have said for centuries. The gathering place seems to bring with it a magic dusting of the sugar of generations past . . . we have fought battles in kitchens, made love in kitchens, and still, we are here three times a day seeking something to feed us. While a beautiful kitchen is to be admired, there is little nourishment from opening the freezer and sticking an anemic meal into our radioactive microwave contraptions (granted, I have an adorable fifties-style microwave, but that's neither here nor there). I humbly submit the idea that we return to the days of fighting battles in kitchens and making love in kitchens and finding deep nourishment in kitchens.

Now don't get your knickers in a bunch, I don't mean actually fighting (heaven knows that happens enough already in kitchens and homes and schools) or actually making love on the kitchen floor (though who am I to say no to that?). I mean fighting the battles of the inner self and how we interact with the world at large. I mean solving inner crises with a cup of tea and a cookie. I mean holding hands at dinner and squeezing at the end of the prayer because life is good and these people around the table . . . they're our people. We're on the same team, fighting the same battles, and we're here, eating the same bread. It is about creating connection. Creating space. There are truly some conversations that can only be had by candlelight at the end of a long lingering dinner. We can look across the dwindling light and ask a friend, "How are you?" and something about a full stomach and the soft glow of a candle melts the barriers we put up for the rest of the world and invites a true response. Things worth having don't come easily, just as sometimes conversations worth having don't come over frozen dinners in front of the laptop. We get enough fear out there in the world. We get enough anxiety driving home. Hang your hat, my dear, at my house. Take your coat off, let me warm you.

Now, I won't pull any punches: Having friends over for dinner is messy. It's one of those funny things in life that is a tangible reflection of our own hearts. It involves a lot of vulnerability, a virtue in short supply these days. Our houses are messy. Our hearts are all aflutter. Our schedules are criss-crossingly dizzying. Yes, yes, and yes. Say yes anyway. Invite anyway. I'll tell you a secret: This is the only life we have. And it is short.

The morning my boyfriend died, I suddenly had a house full of police detectives, medical inspectors, family, friends, and probably a few other strangers who wandered in that I didn't even notice. My house was a mess. I wanted to clean, desperately. I was embarrassed. I was also numb and incapable of any of it. One friend went to the kitchen where she cleaned it top to bottom. It was her way of loving on me and keeping herself busy. I cringed, knowing the state of the mountain of dishes. But I was being interviewed by the deputy. See, life has this funny way of taking control out from under us. People were in my space, because someone very important was missing from it. I gave in. People traipsed in and out of my house for the next month at least, and I learned my lesson: They want to be there. They don't care if I haven't made my bed and I'm still in my pajamas and all I can manage to offer them is to gesture towards the kettle and tell them where the tea is. They want to be there. I will honor that and invite them. Yes, they can be here. Yes, for me. Yes, despite the mess. It's a tough lesson to learn, and one that life decided to teach me, so I can tell you.

Entertaining will also create a literal mess: lots of dishes. Heck, even eating for one is messy! Creating my morning latte makes at least three extra things to wash, but it is all part of the process. Dishes are one of the constants of life. They are also one of the most beautiful parts of life because they are so deeply connected to our present. Dishes come into our lives at least three times a day, and are shared by everyone we love. That becomes even clearer when we've had a few friends over and there is the evidence of life shared in the form of a million dishes. If you have a dishwasher and you can shove them all in, go for it. Life is busy. But I have lived without a dishwasher my entire adult life, and I must say, I am grateful for that. Especially after entertaining, I enjoy the time of reflection and introspection while washing dishes. Chances are you have used at least a few special dishes that need to be hand washed, so enjoy the process. I'm a morning person, so I don't feel stressed by dirty dishes left overnight. I find it a calming ritual to start the morning washing the day's dishes while the tea kettle gets going. I choose my mug for my morning caffeine first, and get it ready before washing dishes. I usually finish washing the dishes at the exact time the kettle sings, which does my heart good, a small victory to start the day. In the afternoon when I come home from work or the day's activities, colorful dishes shining in the sunlight are an uplifting sight that cheers me to cook dinner. But if you can't sleep knowing there are dirty dishes in the sink, by all means make an evening ritual out of it.

I keep two towels on the over-the-cabinet towel rack by the sink: one for hands and one for dishes. The hand towel is always more textured, be it waffled, woven/jacquard, or even terry (since it is just for hands). A good dish-drying towel is thin cotton, preferably a true flour sack towel or unprinted cotton. These will absorb the water and leave no lint. I'm lucky enough to have a stack of flour sack towels my Grandma embroidered with little bunnies doing chores. They make me smile. I also adore my grandmother's aprons. Her pastel Pyrex mixing bowls. Her Hoosier cabinet complete with flour dispenser. The light yellow cracked melamine cup that was a fixture of my childhood, used to gently pour water over my head in the bathtub, now left in the flour bin to scoop. My kitchen is filled with these generational treasures that tug at my heart strings. My aprons hang on a vintage flower hook that barely stands out from my vintage flower wallpaper. If you only saw my kitchen, you might think I am a grandmother myself, instead of just her vintage-loving granddaughter.

My large double porcelain farm sink is framed by old pine cabinets with shelves on the side for my vintage tea tins and jadeite tea cups. The top shelf holds cookbooks, including my reprint of my grandmother's classic Betty Crocker gingham edition. The scene is topped by a carved wood valance. I have a tin sign that says "Nest" above the sink and below the vintage milk-glass sconce that illuminates the work area. Yes, the kitchen, my nest. My feathers-and-string, flour-and-chocolate little heart of the home.

A love of vintage dishes is deep in my heart and a little too deep for my small kitchen's cabinets.

The clean lines of modern design and the cozy nostalgia of days gone by adorn my table and make me happy. While I've borrowed many of these from my grandmother's kitchen cabinets, I simply love scouring thrift and antique stores for pieces that make my heart leap, too.

My kitchen collections:
- Fire King Jadeite
- vintage pink and blue Pyrex of all kinds
- vintage ramekins and pitchers
- vintage table linens
- vintage party supplies
- vintage melamine
- vintage glassware

The Laundry

I love a fresh load of colorful laundry or bright whites. It is so satisfying to the eye. A warm load of blankets fresh from the dryer is always worth at least a few seconds to snuggle them, no matter how pressing other matters may seem.

I find it supremely satisfying to iron linens. To see the wrinkles steam out and disappear, to fold them neatly and stack them beautifully; I feel as if I am the richest woman in the world to have such lovely things and the time to press them. Let's talk about sheets, too. The sensual pleasure of sleeping on freshly ironed sheets is such a simple luxury. It turns your own humble bed into the finest suite in the Plaza. Forget ironing, though, if you must, and get a steamer. I love a good steamer, too. Silks, dresses, and skirts steam up beautifully and the rhythm of steaming garments is another activity that allows one to dream. Hang your wrinkle-free clothes up and admire them. A solid hour's work and your closet sighs a big relief. You are ready to go in the morning. You have accomplished a task and there is visible, tangible improvement in your life. This isn't something that fades into cyberspace; tomorrow when you open your closet they are still there, wrinkle-free as ever, and you'll want to choose a dress that makes you smile. I'm of the opinion that everyone needs a clothing steamer.

Everyone should also have a sweater shaver. Hehe, that name makes me giggle. But these little $10 gadgets can give years of additional life to your sweatshirts, sweaters, and anything else that gets pilled. There's no worry of ruining the garment since the blades are inside the grate on the shaver, so only pills that get sucked inside get trimmed. Of course, don't try this on anything with tassels or on detailed/delicate fabric, but otherwise, shave away.

When it comes to sheets, there are summer sheets and winter sheets. The changing-over is always a moment of special consequence to mark the seasons. Crisp cotton for summer, of course. I love vintage cotton percale sheets, well-worn and with flowers strewn all over them. Other options are pale pink, tiny gingham, or anything girly and sunny. For winter, one cannot live without fleece, flannel, or jersey sheets. These are thicker and stay warm, perfect for cozying up.

A note about folding sheets: For Pete's sake, don't worry about it. If folded bottom sheets make your heart soar, by all means fold them. They do have corners and there are several ways to quickly fold them. But life is short, and I won't be lecturing you to fold sheets unless you so wish.

How to Load a Clothesline

The scent and feel of line-dried linens is unbeatable. I admit I am not a fan of the scratchy line-dried towels (a good snap before and after being on the line helps soften them a bit), but just about anything else carries the sunshine inside to me. First things first with a clothesline: Wipe it down to get rid of dirt and grime (ahem, from the birds flying overhead) that may ruin your fresh clothes. When you're loading a clothesline, you'll want to do this in a certain way to get the best results. I much prefer wooden clothespins because I find them more aesthetically pleasing. Plastic clothespins also have a habit of snapping uncontrollably off the line. Hang pants by the waistbands with the fly open. Hang shirts by the two side seams, upside-down with the arms hanging. Delicates can be hung with one clothespin to keep things discreet. Towels should be folded over an inch or two and held in place with several clothespins. Same with sheets . . . let them fly in that wind and sunshine. Remember to always take your clothespins inside when you're done so they don't rot, and take colorful items in as soon as they dry to minimize fading.

Color and Happy Things

I like a bountiful environment. A lot of happy things. Happy-pretty-messy. Projects galore. Half-written notes, half-read books, half-drunk tea . . . it is the detritus of life. It reminds me that I live here, that coming back to finish things is a privilege, and that a happy place to keep my heart is a blessing.

I am a contradiction in myself most days, so my house is too, as it follows the soul. I like frills and sharp corners. I like polka dots and stripes, wicker and wood, silk and flannel. Most days my bed is unmade. A cocoon—all snuggly, cozy fluff—to make a home for me as I sleep. Other days I find nothing more delightful than the feeling of slipping between freshly washed, ironed sheets and perfectly made bedding, as if I am at a hotel. What a luxury. Both have their place in my home and I embrace this.

To me, color is a neutral. I always say that my interior decorating palette is "color." Color goes with color, and pattern goes with pattern, within reason. But sometimes without reason, too. If I love it, it comes home with me. By nature of being chosen by some part of me, it all works together as a reflection of me.

Happy things are what make a house personal; what make it come alive. I love hunting down little gems that make me smile when I see them. Some may call these dust-collectors but they only collect dust if you let them, only get stale if you let them. I like to constantly rotate my items and décor so that I am not bored and it never becomes "white noise" to my senses. One friend just came to visit and said, "Your apartment is different every time I come over." Another friend calls my apartment the "Natalie Museum" because different and unique things are always on display. A friend's three-year-old came barreling in, looked around and said with a big sigh, "I just *knew* you'd have pretty things!"

Happy Things in My Apartment:
- vintage children's books
- vintage cameras
- jars of watercolors, colored pencils, and various colored pens
- vintage alphabet cards used as wall decorations
- vintage vases, including my "Bunny Butt" vase, which is a bunny vase where you put a plant in his tail-end,

but I use it for my "mad money" stash. I call it "bunny butt money," because why wouldn't I?

- I keep my favorite clothes and shoes on display sometimes, too
- "tablescapes" or table-top displays that coordinate with the seasons
- beautiful cards from friends
- a poster of Jacqueline Kennedy's dresses from the White House years
- a bowl of fresh lemons (the pop of yellow does wonders for the eyes)

I'm a fan of having family photos scattered around the home, but do not approve of a "graveyard" version, where all of the family photos from decades past are on one table or shelf. This type of display is overwhelming and a sure-fire dust-collector. I prefer to update most family photos to current ones as frequently as possible. There is still a high-school photo of me at my worst that is altogether embarrassing and makes me cringe every time I see it at my grandma's. Place photographs strategically on bookshelves, tucked on little displays, tacked on inspiration boards, or framed and hung with various mirrors and art. Incorporate them into your life.

The Art of the Bed

I'm a bed girl. Oh that sounds bad, but it's true. I can't walk by a bed without plopping onto it, I'm a huge fan of long naps, and I find a good bed one of the best things in life.

how to make life beautiful: sleep more

Winter Blanket-Layering 101

The first layer should always be thin and comfortable—either a sheet, light blanket, or the light cotton cover of a duvet. Top sheets are currently out of vogue and tend to end up a tangled mess by the bottom of the bed for some reason, but proper hospital corners should keep things in shape. Then you'll want your

warmest layer. If you have a heating blanket, place it here first, followed by the down comforter to keep all of your body heat (and the heat from the heating blanket) tucked in. Next, I love a thin wool blanket, but this is optional and can go in place of the heating blanket under the down comforter if you want the down comforter and its pretty duvet on top. A quilt tops things off and is usually kept folded at the end of the bed to be added if necessary. A solid down comforter insulated this way should keep you quite cozy indeed.

In Praise of the Down Comforter

A down comforter is one of the best investments you can make in your life, no matter what climate you live in. When I first moved to Vermont, my co-workers knew how freezing I was (I moved here from Florida) and they all chipped in to buy me a down comforter. Ten years later it's still going strong. Not only does it keep me crazy-warm, it is a frothy marshmallow blanket. That may very well be its best quality in my opinion . . . the loft and fluff-factor of a down comforter is unmatched and essential to creating a cozy bed. The puffiness of the down in the baffles (the quilting that keeps the feathers from clumping) makes a bed delightfully inviting. A down comforter is expensive, but it's worth getting the best quality you can afford, and the right weight for your climate. A good bedding shop will have all the details. A summer-weight down comforter in warmer climates is thin but still has loft, and is comforting and altogether lovely. I have a lavender-colored summer down comforter from Pacific Coast. If you are allergic to down, they make fabulous substitutes these days, though nothing is quite as good as the real thing.

Similarly, a down pillow is unbeatable for mash-ability when sleeping and cloud-like comfort. It conforms to any position and cradles with a gentle support. I generally sleep with one down pillow and one firm pillow. I'd love to have a feather-bed topper to go on top of my mattress, but alas, that luxury has eluded me in life so far. I have no doubt that this would make my bed even more comfortable and I would probably never go out in public again.

The Summer Bed

As I mentioned, there are winter sheets and summer sheets. The base layer for a summer bed is cool and crisp summer sheets. The next step is a lightweight quilt or a summer-weight down comforter. To top it off, I love a vintage chenille bedspread. These are barely bedspreads at all, merely coverings that are often folded down to the bottom during the night. They can be bought new, but are also plentiful (if expensive) in antique and thrift stores. The chenille patterns are generally floral in nature and white-on-white. A colored chenille bedspread, if you can find one, is tops for summer, though. I love even more pillows than usual as well. They make for great nap companions and liven up otherwise sparse warm-weather bed linens.

Making or Messing Up the Bed

As mentioned earlier, I love both versions of the bed, both beautifully made and welcomingly messy. Giving the down comforter a good-old fluff-snap is fun before bed, and especially fun if you're in the bed while someone else is fluff-snapping it and letting it float down over you. I giggle at this like a child, and beg for it to be done a few times before I am tucked in. Perhaps you have a rule that you make the bed during the week and keep it unmade on the weekends. I like this idea, I do. A made bed at the end of a long workday soothes the soul and creates a moment of organization in the brain before bedtime. Yes, the bed is made. Life can't be all that bad, right? Slipping between the sheets, you can let go of the day's offenses and ease into dreaming. On the weekend, though, a messy bed invites lingering, invites crumbs from a breakfast tray, invites snuggling and kicking covers around and staying in bed till noon. I am a fan of all of these things, indeed.

A Bed-Nap

A bed-nap is a different animal than the couch- or chair-nap. It is the most luxurious version, the most sensual and the most frequent nap in my world. Of course it is called a bed-nap in my vernacular because it is taken in bed,

under the covers. This may or may not involve pajamas or the stripping of uncomfortable clothing, but it usually does. There's
just something wrong about wearing jeans in
bed, don't you think? Get comfortable, snuggle
in, and give yourself a full three hours. For some

reason, that's almost always exactly how long my bed-naps take, and one of
the biggest reasons they are such a luxury. I know, I know, I know. You don't
think you have three hours. If this feels extravagant to you, start small and
work your way up from a catnap. Find your natural nap equilibrium. But Sunday afternoon was made for bed-napping, and I will almost always choose
this over any other Sunday afternoon activity. If you have a family, make this
a family ritual where everyone naps or enjoys quiet time. When you wake,
it's time for your three o'clock coffee or tea, imagine that! These naps are
soothing no matter the season. In summer, I adore the windows open, a quiet
breeze lifting the curtains gently and lulling me to sleep, the sunshine keeping
me warm and safe. In spring or fall, a rainy afternoon makes resisting my bed
nearly impossible. A winter afternoon when the clouds are low and bringing
snow is practically ordering me to take a bed-nap. If I'm healthy, I always wake
quite refreshed from a bed-nap. If I'm not feeling up to par, a bed-nap can
make me feel lethargic the rest of the afternoon, but this is only because my
body is craving more sleep. In that case, I set up with a book or movie and
some hot tea and stay in bed. Body knows best.

A Good Night's Sleep

A good night's sleep (and a good life, in my opinion) is all about activating all
of the senses.

When it comes to **touch**, or snuggling, I can't lie: I still sleep with a
teddy bear. I think we do ourselves a disservice to think grown-ups can't
have teddy bears. There is an art to finding a good teddy bear, and it's one
I have perfected. It must have beads in its bottom, a tubby tummy, ful-

ly flexible arms and legs, a snuggly head that makes a good chin rest, be the exact right snuggling size, and exude a personality that speaks to you. This is tough to find, but Ganz and Mary Meyer rarely let me down. Anyway, besides a super fluffy bed filled with down comforters and pillows, a teddy bear is my next bedroom accessory for a good night's sleep. Even if you sleep with a partner, you can still sleep with a teddy bear. I know several friends who do, I promise. Boys have gotten around this stigma by snuggling with sweatshirts or tee shirts they abandon in the night and these are a good substitute. But I also happen to know several grown boys who sleep with teddy bears . . . *shhh*.

Getting warm is important, but don't get too warm. I like to keep my bedroom cool, perhaps even with a fan to keep the air circulating, and then have plenty of blankets. Stale air does not inspire sleep.

For **taste**, a traditional nightcap does wonders for a good night's sleep. There is a reason they call it a nightcap, as a little dose keeps dreams sweet and sleep deep. Port is my favorite, in a vintage port glass. In the winter, a nice boozy hot chocolate does the trick too, though I'll enjoy that a little earlier in the evening. People say warm milk with butter is excellent for this, too, but the thought of warm milk makes me cringe.

A calming **scent**, such as lavender, vanilla, or rose, can be sprayed on the pillow or diffused into the air to bring soothing sleep.

Sight is a bit of a silly one, because at night what we actually want is no sight, with a very dark room. Of course, keep those electronics out of the bedroom for at least half an hour before bed. Grab a book instead, or journal. This allows the brain to wind down without the blaring blue light of social media screaming, "stay awake." If you can wear a darling little sleep mask, please do. I find them alluring but haven't been able to keep one on for anything.

An appropriate level of **sound** is important for good sleep. Many people like to sleep with a white noise machine, fan, or ear plugs to block out any noises.

Set the environment, take a few deep breaths, snuggle down into your down (ha), and count your blessings.

Waking Up Well

"WHEN YOU WAKE UP, WAKE UP!" — THE SOUND OF MUSIC

Waking up is the hardest part of having a fabulous bed. Even if my brain wants to get going, sometimes my body is too attached to comfort. I tumble out of bed and turn on a warm-yellow light first thing. Then I slip into my slippers and blink my eyes a bunch of times and roll my neck a few times on my way into the kitchen. Like many, the thought of coffee and breakfast is what gets me out of bed most days. But no matter how cozy the bed is, waking up well is of paramount importance. It cannot be overstated that the first hour or so of your day greatly impacts the rest of it.

As I mentioned earlier, I like to get the kettle going, get my coffee cup ready, then wash any dishes left from the night before. Before I wash the dishes though, I turn on my vintage kitchen radio. The real-ness of a vintage radio—that comforting crackling over the airwaves—does my heart good. I dance a little as I wash the dishes, listen to the fourth graders do the morning weather report from the local school, and wake myself up for the day. It is one of my favorite routines.

In the winter, my bathroom is frequently cold, so I'll turn on the heater while I eat my breakfast to warm it up. In winter, my breakfast is almost always oatmeal, and in the summer, almost always yogurt and granola or overnight oats.

Winter Oatmeal for One

½ cup water
½ cup milk
½ cup old-fashioned oats
1 tablespoon cashew or almond butter
Sprinkle of raw cacao nibs
Sprinkle of flax seeds or chia seeds
Dash of cinnamon
Optional additions: raisins, chopped apple, or nuts

In a small saucepan on the stove, bring the water and milk to a gentle boil. Stir in the oats. Reduce heat to medium and stir occasionally for approx. 5 minutes or until most of the liquid is absorbed. Transfer to a bowl and top with the cashew or almond butter, cacao nibs, seeds, cinnamon, and any additional toppings you desire.

Summer Overnight Oats for One

½ cup milk
½ cup banana, raspberry, or vanilla yogurt
½ cup old-fashioned oats
Glug of maple syrup
Toppings of choice, including fruit, cacao nibs, nuts, nut butters, seeds, etc.

Mix well, cover, and refrigerate overnight. It's that easy, and it uses one measuring cup and one spoon. In the morning, top it up! I usually do banana, chocolate-covered cacao nibs, and sunflower nut butter, but I switch it up sometimes. Try adding jam or dried fruit, fresh berries, or anything else you can come up with!

While I eat my breakfast and drink my coffee or tea, I'll spend time reading my Bible and devotional and praying before I start my day. This centers me. If I have time, a bit of exercise makes a big difference in my day's energy levels, too. Then it's into the shower and into the day with joy.

Caffeinating/Cooking

The Ritual of Hot Beverages

A hot beverage is so satisfying. We take a sip and drink it deeply, into the cold and downtrodden spaces of ourselves. With each sip we commune with ourselves on a deeper level. We drink a nurturing embrace.

The ritual of a hot beverage is soul-soothing. We realize we could use that elusive *something*, so we choose a hot beverage for its warming, calming, or enticing possibilities. If we need coziness and sweetness, we may reach for warmed apple cider or hot chocolate. If we need contemplation and companionship, we may select tea. Should we feel sluggish and uninspired, coffee may be the beverage of choice. Consciously or subconsciously, we reach for a drink that suits our sensibilities and needs at that moment.

If we're at home, we select a mug. Some days I want the solid red mug. Other days, I want the dainty, gold-rimmed teacup. Sometimes I want one with a pithy saying, a cute cartoon animal, or a sophisticated pattern. If we're out at a coffee shop, we select a paper cup so we can walk in contemplation, or perhaps we feel the need to sit on a wooden chair near the window and stare at the old brick buildings, so we say "for here." All of this, too, speaks from our souls.

It takes a repetitive, heartening motion to dunk a tea bag. We might decide to stir a spoonful of caramel sauce into our apple cider, or go for the whipped cream this time. I curl my hand around the cup, be it fancy or simple, paper or porcelain, and I already feel comforted. Here, in my hand, is warmth and a small dose of the knowledge that everything will be okay.

We drink deeply and transport ourselves, for a moment, to another place. These moments are fleeting, to be sure, but they speak of very profound things. We ourselves need an infusion of comfort and inspiration.

Next time you drink your coffee or other hot beverage, sip it lovingly, in good health and well-being, filling yourself with its metaphorical soul-healing qualities. No matter where you are, even if it's with a commuter mug in the pickup line at school, imbibe with the knowledge that the aroma, the warmth, and the taste are filling your senses and relaxing your sympathies. We may not read tea leaves, but we can find much wisdom in a warm beverage.

Tea: My First Love

There is something about a first love that never leaves you. I'm not sure what hole is in our hearts for "first love" but it's there, we all know it. Tea is and always will have the distinction of being my first (hot beverage) love. As a girl, I was enthralled with tea parties and the rituals of white gloves, vintage hats, pearls, and pinkies up. Pansies on porcelain cups, petit fours . . . oh it's quite pleasing. I've always relished a good tea, be it at The Drake in downtown Chicago at Christmastime, or at a bed-and-breakfast in northern Minnesota. The first trip I ever took overseas was to  England, and as a ten-year-old tea connoisseur, I felt quite grown-up. Tea is deceptively simple in America. We grab a box out of the cabinet and dunk a tea bag in microwaved water. Oh no, my friends. Tea is so much more. Loose-leaf teas will open up a whole new world to you. All you need is one little $1 gadget: A tea strainer. Scoop up 1–2 teaspoons of tea per cup in the ball and let it steep for 3 minutes. If you want to adjust the strength of your tea, adjust how much tea you add, not how long you let it steep or it will become bitter. Herbal teas can steep longer, 5–15 minutes. I like my tea black, but it does go down easy with a dash of cream or milk, a splash of lemon and a sprinkle of sugar. Tea has a unique dual personality in that it can be sloshed down in three cups before you even know what's happened, as if your body needed it for fortification against the shocks of the world's ways. Or you can sip it slowly, contemplatively, breathing in the poetry of its steam and finding that it soothes the lining of your inner being.

I know fancy tea doesn't usually come in tea bags (though this is changing), but truth is, I feel slightly cheated when I don't get an inspiring quote with my hot beverage. I'm quite pleased to find those on boxes, tins, or tags on tea bags.

Tea, as in the verb of *having tea*, requires a bit more fancy. The little saucer under a tea cup simply begs for a sweet. Indulge it. A tray makes things much better, even if it's going to sit on your coffee table or kitchen table. Better yet, bring it to the porch, bring it to the floor in the back of the closet if that's what the day requires, or to the side of the bathtub. Bring a little candle, and light it, for Pete's sake. Is there a flower in your  house or yard? It belongs on your tray. Bring a little dish of honey and a slice of lemon to add to your tea when you've arrived at your destination. A book or fresh magazine tucked under the tray does wonders, too. I love the smell of a new magazine, don't you? Something about it is intoxicating, especially through the veiled scent of a delicious Darjeeling steam. How luxurious.

Coffee: My True Love

Oh, oh coffee, how I adore you and your caffeine-crazy-inducing ways. I haven't always known I would be a coffee lover, but it was always there, deep in my Swedish blood, waiting for me to grow up enough to enjoy the taste.

Like many, I was eased into coffee with the sweet-cold Frappuccino drink as a teenager, giddy to go out for adult coffee with friends. For my thirteenth birthday party, I had a fancy coffee party in a neighborhood coffee shop, and felt oh-so-very grown-up, even though I was barely drinking coffee. College passed without much more interest in coffee, until I hit graduate school. Graduate school will drive a person to many vices, and for me, it was a deadline-fueled interest in anything caffeinated.

My mother, grandmother, and grandfather were all around-the-clock coffee drinkers, straight up or with a dash of sugar. Usually percolated on the stove in an old-fashioned camp-style coffee pot that is the sound and scent of my childhood. In Sweden, there is a tradition called "Fika" which is similar to a British tea break. At 3 p.m., families gather with sweets and coffee to discuss the day and find a little inspiration in liquid energy to face the rest of it.  A fancy Fika can have as many as seven different "courses" of desserts, but generally it is a simple sweet roll topped with crunchy sugar and enjoyed with a black coffee.

Coffee is not merely a part of Swedish culture, or American Starbucks culture. Tradition runs deeply through Cuban coffee, Turkish coffee, Viennese coffee, and in many other parts of the world. My Swedish mother practically bleeds coffee. She found it so intriguing she even paints with coffee and built her entire art career around it. So I come by my obsession honestly, though later in life.

When I finally decided I liked coffee, it was still with cream and sugar, but it was present, strong, intoxicating, and full of possibility. I'm not going to lie, the thing that propelled me into embracing my Swedish roots was far more miserly than any real maternal affection: I didn't want to buy cream for my coffee anymore. I weaned myself off adding anything to my coffee, except for on special occasions or in espresso-based drinks.

I think that is what it takes to enjoy the espresso-based drinks: an appreciation for coffee in its natural form, naked and free of cloyingly sweet masks. While you may find it tastes like dirt at first, give it a chance. Like chocolate, it is a different animal when unsweetened and the slight bitterness is part of the appeal. Granted, properly brewed coffee is not bitter but smooth, but to our unaccustomed palates it will taste bitter until we appreciate the aroma and neutrality of the drink.

Then, and only then, will espresso begin to appeal. A shot of espresso is a friend for the lonely. When I was in Paris, I saw this first-hand. Espresso is also a friend for the croissant, especially if it is chocolate-filled. Everyone, lonely at the start of their day, in workaday clothes and with a placid demeanor, comes to the espresso bar for their daily constitutional: a demitasse, thrown back, of pure dark liquid that chases away the night.

Slowly but surely we need our old friend throughout the day, less in your face, and softened around the edges. Give us a little steamed milk, a little foam for a spring in our step through the afternoon. Give us a little chocolate if the day calls for it; give us a little whipped cream if we can afford the frivolity.

Coffee is a lifestyle, a heritage, a part of our daily life that never gets old.

Dictionary of Espresso Drinks

Americano: Espresso served with hot water to approximate an American coffee overseas. This is actually a delicious and distinctly different drink than regular drip coffee, and is one of my favorites to order in a café.

Café au Lait: Coffee with steamed milk, usually served in France. Not my favorite, since it just tastes like a weak latte to me (which it is, since there is no espresso involved).

Café Breve: A latte made with half milk and half cream, or half-and-half. Tasty, tasty, tasty.

Café Latte: Espresso and steamed milk, usually whole milk. The new daily drink in America. Does anyone order plain coffee anymore? Just kidding. A latte is generally ⅓ espresso and ⅔ milk with a bit of foam on the top for good measure and a chance to be fancy with some latte art. I tend to make mine a bit stronger.

Cappuccino: ⅓ espresso, ⅓ milk, and ⅓ milk foam. Usually has a cap of foam that extends over the top of the cup and keeps the coffee beneath hot. I love drinking through the foam cap of a cappuccino. Can be ordered "dry" without the milk, as only espresso and foam.

Con Panna: Means "with whipped cream" and can be added to any espresso drink or plain espresso.

Crema: The golden bubble "cap" that is created on proper espresso. Insulates the espresso from the air and helps with latte art. "Café crema" is also a vintage (1940s–50s) name for a simple espresso.

Demitasse: The name for the small espresso cup that holds one shot or ounce of espresso.

Flat White: A new drink to us Americans (thanks, Starbucks) and relatively new in general, the Flat White was developed in the 1970s in

New Zealand as a cross-over between the latte and the frothier cappuccino. The flat white occasionally has an extra shot of espresso and the milk is more velvety and less foamed (hence, flat, as opposed to the capped cappuccino).

Macchiato: A macchiato is an espresso shot "marked" with milk foam. Can be served with a dash of cocoa powder on top.

Mocha: A mocha or café mocha is a chocolate latte, with ⅔ espresso, ⅓ steamed milk, and the addition of chocolate syrup or chocolate powder.

Shot: A shot of espresso or flavored syrup is one ounce. Hence, a "double-shot" drink has two shots, or two ounces, of espresso or flavoring. A typical small or medium drink will have two shots of espresso, and larger sizes would have three shots. You'd probably have to request a fourth, or "quad," if you wanted it in a larger drink (hello caffeine crazy!).

The list of variations and regional spins is pretty much endless, but these are the basic espresso-based drinks that you could order. As you can see, these are all created without sugar. Of course, a coffeehouse syrup-flavored latte will have plenty of sugar, and you can always add it if you like. But the slight sweetness of the steamed milk creates a pleasing drink that is still neutral to the palate. That's one of my favorite things about espresso-based drinks, actually, and why they go effortlessly with additional sweets. They can also be sweet enough to keep you on a sugar high for days if you add flavored syrups, maple syrup, honey, and/or whipped cream. All have their place in a repertoire.

The At-Home Version

LET'S TALK INGREDIENTS

Since a latte is simple, it is imperative that the ingredients be top notch. Since we are doing this at home, we can't have professional level of everything, but I'm going to give you the list of what I have found creates the best latte at home, easily.

ESPRESSO

This is the most basic component. Coffee creates a weak latte. Trust me; I spent a year of mornings experimenting with making my coffee stronger to "fake" espresso. It doesn't work, and you'll be disappointed with the results. In fact, it's not even a latte—at that point, it's just a *cafe au lait*, which, let's be honest, isn't the same.

> *Instant espresso:* I have to admit, this is my go-to. It makes my life simple. I keep a jar of Bustelo instant espresso in my cabinet at all times and a small 1 tsp. scoop handy. I will say that instant espresso can be hard to locate. I went to three stores before finding a jar in my town.
>
> *Stovetop espresso:* A stovetop espresso pot makes good espresso, but it is murkier than instant espresso and more bitter. It's supposedly better for creating a gorgeous crema for latte art, but I haven't been able to create this coveted crema any better than with my jar of instant granules. It also takes longer, and while the pot is quite gorgeous in your kitchen, they are often made from aluminum and can leave a metallic taste. I haven't found it worth the effort and ended up giving my pot away.
>
> *Countertop espresso machine:* This is my second-favorite way to make espresso, and if I have a few extra minutes I'll choose this over instant. I've used various inexpensive countertop espresso machines (i.e., Mr. Coffee's $20 espresso machine) and these are great for beginners, and if you like to have one sitting on your counter to look fancy (don't worry,

I won't judge). If you are spending for a machine anyway, research and get one with a pump/pressure system instead of simply a steam system. It will mean a bit more money, but the difference is astounding and it needn't be nearly as expensive as the "big and fancy machine" below. I also love my sleek, red single-serve Nespresso machine.

Big and fancy machine: If you have a fancy machine and can pull double shots of espresso in your sleep, by all means, please go ahead and make me one, too. But I live in a small apartment with limited resources and counter space. Staring at a complicated machine in the morning makes my brain go back to sleep. Side note: The purchase of these several-thousand-dollar machines sometimes signals a mid-life crisis, so beware.

The complicated way: I once heard of someone who went to their local coffee shop down the street each morning to purchase a shot of espresso to then bring home and "make" a latte at home. I find this laughable for many reasons . . . but at least she was supporting the local economy. Let's make our espresso at home, or buy your drink at the coffee shop.

MILK

The second most important part of a latte. I've experimented a lot with various milks and find that good old 2% or whole milk does the best job for me. Feel free to experiment on your own. Here is the basic run down.

Skim/1%: This will give you a lot of foam, which is good for beginners, but the resulting latte will be too full of air and big bubbles instead of a nice microfoam like we want.

2%: My favorite. This is my everyday milk, and the fact that I don't have to buy anything separate for my lattes makes my life a lot easier. Creates beautifully layered microfoam.

Café Latte, Whole: Whole milk is my second favorite and what is generally used to create a latte. It creates a rich and luscious drink.

Café Breve, Half and Half or Light Cream: Oh my. Here we are talking about something totally different than latte territory and it's quite sinfully delicious.

Soy Milk: Works decently; creates foam that falls flat and dissipates into big bubbles, but will taste nice, though different.

Almond Milk: Works decently, though the flavor and texture are different and it can taste burnt if overheated.

OTHER EQUIPMENT

AeroLatte: This is my tool of choice for texturizing milk to create a nice steamed quality without the steaming wand found on high end machines. Easily found and only about $20, these take up very little countertop space, are easily washed, and even kids enjoy using them to make foamed milk for Mom and Dad.

Pitcher for Milk: If you're using a machine, you can purchase a small stainless steel pitcher designed specifically to be used with the steaming wand on your machine. If you're going my shortcut way and will be microwaving the milk, please do not use stainless steel! A small, glass 1-cup Pyrex liquid measure will work perfectly for this. You want your milk pitcher to be an actual pitcher with a spout for easy pouring.

CHOOSING A MUG

A good coffee mug insulates the drink and keeps it warm longer, which is why stoneware is preferable over porcelain. Thin china may look lovely but you'll be sad when your coffee is cold. A wide bowl on the mug makes it go cold more quickly, except in the case of a stoneware cappuccino mug, where the cap of foam insulates the top of the drink while the stoneware insulates the sides. Look for a solid handle that fits comfortably and can be enveloped to keep your hands warm. Don't forget to test the lip (rim) of the mug too. Stoneware mugs have wider lips because of the thicker nature of the material.

A thick lip takes a bit of getting used to, and might cause some spilling in the meantime, but I find it comforting and solid.

Then, of course, mood factors in. When I was younger, I thought it was preferable to have all matching mugs. It seemed proper, yes? Then I realized the importance of mood in drinking coffee. It is intimately tied with the start of our day, or is the "reset button" of a day gone awry. The vessel is just as important as the drink. Now I keep a set of matching mugs, but they are at the back of the cabinet and rarely used.

I keep mugs from travels, from friends, with sayings that make me smile, and with patterns that cheer me up. I like stoneware mugs from World Market, Pier 1, and the souvenir shops at the National Parks; real diner mugs from my favorite diners; and vintage mugs from my thrift store's quarter shelf. I'm never entirely sad when a mug gets broken because it is an excuse to find a new one. Rotate mugs regularly so you're always on your toes in the morning and can find one that matches your mood.

For iced coffee, you'll want a double-wall insulated tumbler with a reusable straw. These are almost exclusively plastic. Be sure to look for BPA-free plastic. Tervis Tumblers are my favorite; they're heavy-duty, gorgeous, and made in Florida, just down the road from where I lived for many years. Hand wash with a soft sponge to keep the plastic free of scratches and away from the heat of your dishwasher. You can use a glass jar with a drinking lid or straw lid, but beware that the glass jars get sweaty and slippery (i.e., dangerous) quickly! I do have a coffee cup converter and straw lid for my mason jars, and I've created a rubber-backed Velcro-on sleeve for it to prevent accidents.

As far as pitchers go for making and storing the iced coffee, a gallon storage jug and a gallon pitcher to steep the coffee in overnight will do you just fine. I highly prefer glass for anything kept in the fridge because it keeps the beverages much colder and I quite like the vintage look. A pour spout is necessary, and a nice little spigot is even handier for grab-and-go coffee.

Everyday Favorite Honey Latte

This is my daily double shot latte in cold weather. I love the touch the honey gives . . . just a little bit of smooth sweetness and a dose of the daily allergy-fighting and cold-fighting goodness that comes from local honey. Of course, you can leave the honey out if you prefer and I do that frequently, too.

2 tsp. instant espresso

⅓ cup milk

1 tsp. high-quality, raw local honey

Boil fresh, filtered water. While that comes to a boil, place your instant espresso in the bottom of the mug you'll be drinking from. When the water is ready, pour it over the espresso until your cup is about ½ full. Pour the milk into a small glass measuring cup with a pouring spout (a Pyrex) and microwave for 1 minute and 40 seconds, approximately, or until hot and steaming. Get your jar of honey out, pour a generous teaspoon of honey into the hot espresso, and stir to dissolve. Then use your spoon to skim off the foam that will have formed on your hot milk. Discard. Using an AeroLatte kept well under the surface of the milk, texturize the hot milk until it is velvety, rich, and nearly doubled. Quickly pour it into the espresso, leaving the foam for the end and swirling gently to create a pattern if you wish. Drink immediately.

Everyday Favorite Iced Coffee

This is my everyday go-to in the summer months when even the thought of turning on the kettle makes me overheat. I like my coffee quite strong, so feel free to adjust the amounts here to your liking. The process is incredibly simple and perfectly suited for summer's laid-back schedule.

12 ounces high quality coffee
1 gallon cold, filtered water

Pour the coffee in the bottom of a 1 gallon or larger pitcher. Pour in the cold water and stir to saturate all of the grounds. Refrigerate overnight. Strain into your storage jug through a fine mesh strainer lined with a single layer of paper towel to catch all the grounds. Store in the refrigerator.

EXTRAS

Drink that iced coffee straight, or doctor it up a bit with some cream and simple syrup (simply heat equal amounts of water and sugar until the sugar is dissolved; let cool and add to coffee to sweeten). You can make ice cubes out of your left-over coffee, but I actually prefer the fresh addition of water ice cubes. As long as your coffee is cold-brewed, water ice cubes won't alter the taste significantly.

Coffee Shops for Creativity

While making coffee at home is one of my favorite daily rituals, I do love a good 2 p.m. Tuesday coffee date with a friend. The music of the hum and grind of rattling espresso machines is rousing. A round two-person table commonly found in coffee shops adds extra warmth. I adore the convergence of humanity and days intersecting that one finds at a coffee shop. We are all there seeking something necessary: caffeine. And with it we find an extra splash of life. The people watching alone is worth the extra $3 you spend on your coffee. Different coffee shops have different vibes, and I like to vary the experience. I once found a thrift shop with an attached coffee shop and live music venue. I just about moved in. But instead I bought a s'mores latte and almost died of happiness.

Not a Coffee Snob

If you haven't figured it out yet, as much as I love coffee, I'm not a coffee snob. I enjoy coffee from McDonald's (99 cents and I'm there), the gas station (hello Banana Cream Cappuccino from the machine!), the church basement (though not nearly strong enough), and I'm sure I would enjoy the fanciest coffee bar Seattle has to offer (though I've never been to Seattle). If it is caffeinated, I'm there. There is a lot of stress that goes into being a snob about anything and I just don't have enough bandwidth to stress over my coffee. Coffee makes me happy, so why add hurdles to that? If you feel like being a coffee snob goes with your persona, by all means, have at it. As for me and my Arabica beans, they're just fine if they come from a Folgers can, a Via packet, or a drive-through window. If you've just handed me hot coffee, we are best friends. Besides, bad coffee now and again makes spending $5 on a latte an extra special indulgence that I enjoy exceedingly.

The Wooden Spoon and the Table

These are, to me, the two most important aspects of a kitchen. They are also two of the most basic: The workhorses that do everything thanklessly every day. The feel of a good wooden spoon is undeniable. It feels at home in your hand, with a nice heft but not too much, that is evenly weighted within the spoon, much like a good pen feels. I prefer a rectangular handle. Though harder to find, it is easier to grip. I like an elongated, oval-shaped bowl. All of my wooden utensils are from Whetstone Wood-enware in the idyllic little town of Silver Lake, Indiana. I went there once when I was a kid with my mom and brother for a fall festival and to see the house of Billy Sunday, a well-known evangelist. His little Craftsman  home on the lake is adorable, and the kettle corn from the fall fair across the street equally memorable. But most of all, I remember the booth of the hand-crafted maple utensils that John makes on Main Street. I have collected almost the full range of his utensils. From the bench knife to the cookie scoop, the biscuit cutters and old-fashioned potato mashers, to the classic wooden spoon and the stir-fry paddles, they are the very best and I haven't found a rival yet.

Don't even think of buying the cheap 3-pack of spoons at the big box store. These disappointments will give you splinters and warp and crack at the first sign of water. Worse yet are the plastic ones that break and melt without warning. A good wooden spoon, well taken care of, will literally wear away before it cracks or warps. Give them a good coating of mineral oil now and again to keep them in tip-top shape and always hand-wash immediately and air dry. Never soak or bleach your cherished woodenware.

Of course, you'll need to find the perfect container for your wooden spoons. This is tricky because it must be tall enough to support the long handles, but wide enough to contain the various spouts and bowls of the spoons. A unique vessel is often much more appealing than a stainless steel tube from Target that is made to hold utensils. You'll know it when you find it: an antique pitcher, a perfectly sized wide-mouth canning jar, or a re-purposed orchid pot (as my current one is). I have a honeycomb silicone hot pad under my canister to keep it from moving across the counter. This means that I always know where at least one hot pad is, which is not always the case for the everyday use ones.

As for a table, it's all about history. This doesn't necessarily mean you need to get an antique table, but at least one with the potential to become an antique. No particle board furniture allowed in the kitchen. The kitchen table is where so much of life happens. You'll need a table that bears that burden and honor beautifully and with pride. I'm not talking fancy or big. I'm not talking scrolled legs and upholstered chairs you never dare sit on. I'm talking sturdy, real wood, simple, homespun, heavy, capable of accepting wet glasses and cat paws and baby mouths. I'm talking a hand-me-down table with all its bumps and bruises. I grew up with a round cream-colored farm table with a sturdy base and a leaf for entertaining. It had four chairs nightly and six with the leaf. It was bought from a proper furniture store as soon as my parents had enough money. It replaced their hand-me-down table that by that point became an art table, and it saw every meltdown and after-school snack I had all the way to my twenty-first birthday (I still have "after-school snacks" at 3 p.m., don't you?). There may be times in your life where a family table makes your heart heavy. But don't despair. Instead, fill it. Invite others to partake with you, and tell the stories of the bumps and bruises that wood has suffered. Make new bumps and bruises. Be present at your table.

● ● ● ● ● ● ● ● ● ● ● ● ● ●

They tell me that I live with too many hot air balloons

That take me up, up, up, and

I never know where they will set me down

They say that's a bad thing, that going somewhere

Without direction is like going to class without a pen

I never was fond of ink; it stakes its claim too quickly

I have a shop for tinkering and puttering and for

Devising maps in pink chalk on the giant blackboard

I stockpile gears and pulleys and ropes and ladders

And paintbrushes and gold frames

There is a whole wall of clocks here, because I am the sort

Who can look at a clock and see only

That it is a curious device, and beautiful too

Should any of you darlings find yourselves in a daring mood

Come away with me, and I'll show you the architecture of

Seeing with daydream eyes, and living with a daydream heart

It looks rather like building a cabin in the sky

One with the finest history and a pennant on the wall

From before we were born:

First Annual Cloud Canoe Champions

I have stacks of magazines, reams of paper, climbing rope

I store ideas in abandoned balloon baskets, covered over with cat hair

And coffee cups

Parachute cloth of every color

Hangs from the rafters should I ever wish to free fall

And I very well may, some glorious day

Just for the thrill of landing softly in a field of wild lupine

They tell me I live with too many

Hot air balloons

But there is a sign on the door of my tinker-shop that says

"Free Rides."

On Being Brave and Baking

I've been a baker my whole life, as well as a writer. I don't know where my love of baking came from. Maybe it skipped a few generations because I hear my great-grandma Emma was a great baker. My grandma knows how to bake up a mean batch of Pillsbury cinnamon rolls, but that's about the extent of it. And even the "pop" of a Pillsbury can scares my mom. So the fact that I checked out every single cookbook in the elementary school library at least a few times is perhaps a bit odd. I remember a few favorites: a *1001 Cookies* tome, the *Nancy Drew Cookbook* (how they managed to make a mystery series for children into a cookbook I'll never know) and the *Boxcar Children Cookbook* (again, how?).

This fascination was not merely curiosity with the books themselves—it extended into the kitchen. When I was eleven I was left home alone while my family went to my brother's baseball game. Mom called me to check in and asked what I was doing. "Making bagels!" I chirped. She balked, half terrified I was boiling bagels on the stove alone and half mystified I even had the gumption to do such a thing. If you name it, I baked it by the time I was seventeen. Lefse, croissants, pita pockets, French bread, puff pastry . . . I was a thirteen-year-old making layered palmiers and pastry cream. At fifteen I had a baking stand at the local farmers' market. My goal my entire life has been to write books and own a bakery.

Then I was diagnosed as gluten intolerant at age eighteen. How is that possible for a baker like me, who sometimes eats six freshly-baked muffins before 9 a.m.? Oh wait, I might be able to see how that's possible. I felt everything I had built up until that point in my life was dashed into a million little pieces and I had to create a new dream. How do you do that? At that point, I was still learning. My heart was broken and I didn't bake for almost three years.

I went the writing direction and avoided the tasteless, offensive imitation baked goods labeled "gluten-free." I finished my college degree in creative writing and went to get a Master's in Poetry. Over the course of those years, gluten-free really took off in the marketplace and there were actually pre-mixed flours on the shelves and decent prepared products. My heart healed a little, and I started experimenting. I liked what I was tasting. My dreams were alive again. I moved back to Minnesota with a Subaru packed to the hilt with all of my baking pans, my pink Swedish clogs, and a "Minnesota or Bust" sign all visible in the windows. People at a Wendy's in Indiana said, "You're a long way from home." Yes, sometimes brave looks like being a long way from home. Sometimes brave looks like challenging the suspension on your car, and your very own sanity, for 3,000 miles. Sometimes brave looks like pulling into Grandma's in Minnesota on an October day just as it starts snowing.

And sometimes being brave means realizing that you don't have enough money to start your dream in a big city. Being brave means putting it back on the burner farthest from your reach and taking a job managing a clothing boutique. Sometimes being brave means giving your heart a break. Sometimes being brave means tucking that dream away for the dentist's chair (you know, as your happy place while you stare into the big white light and hope not to die). And being brave when it is hardest is the place where you grow the most. Your dreams gain layers, experience, and stories. Our identities are fluid. When I hadn't baked for three years because I was devastated by having to be gluten-free, I was still a baker. I was just gaining back my belief. I will be a baker yet, whether that means another farmers' market stand, a full-fledged bakery, or simply a happy circle of friends.

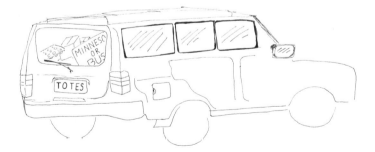

Style and Beauty

I said it in the home section and I'll say it again—my style tends to go one of two ways: I'm a sweatshirt-and-sweatpants girl and a to-the-nines girl. I always have been. When I was in graduate school, I made a commitment to myself to dress like an adult for every class, which helped me master a uniform for the workaday grind. But if you need advice on the best sweatpants or the best red-carpet look, I'm your girl. I have more cozy clothes and cocktail dresses than "real" clothes, and I embrace this dichotomy.

Here is my style secret: confidence. I know it sounds clichéd but I'm 100% serious. You can rock anything with confidence. Dollar store clothing can be stunning on a girl who carries it well and smiles. That is not a function of form, but one of fearlessness, a fact of embracing oneself and existing as a whole. Enjoying life, regardless of what one is wearing, creates a freedom of self that radiates to others.

Aside from that, style is all about mixing the classics with your own flair. I love vintage, but not costume-y vintage. I don't do pearls, full vintage hair and makeup, thigh highs, vintage hats, white gloves, vintage purse, and vintage shoes all at once. For me, that's too much. Modern-vintage, though, that's the stuff. Take one vintage element and mix it up. A 1950s hat looks stunning with today's floaty skater dresses. A 1970s hand-knit sweater is gorgeous with today's liquid leggings. As long as the elements are similar and the look cohesive to your eye, mix it up, darling.

Sweatshirt-and-Shorts Days

"Sweatshirt-and-shorts" is a Minnesota thing—actually, it's a weather phrase more than a fashion one. A sweatshirt-and-shorts day is ideal in Minnesota, especially on the North Shore of Lake Superior. It means the sun is shining and a breeze is coming off the Lake. It's divine, a day to be envied by anyone living anywhere else. Sweatshirts and shorts are ideal because you get to wear the leg-freeing shorts of summer and keep the coziness of the sweatshirt. Coziness is always tops on

my list of priorities. It is such a cabin-y look, and reminds me of "The Parent Trap" movie. Both versions, the Hayley Mills version and the Lindsey Lohan-while-she-was-still-cute version, are two of my favorite movies. I obsessed over the outfits in these movies, made lists of them, and even tried to get my mom to send me to the summer camp where the Lohan version was filmed. Anyway, the campy outfits remind me of sweatshirt-and-shorts days, minus fencing duels and twin capers.

My Favorite Fashion Movies

The Parent Trap, both the Hayley Mills (1961) and Lindsey Lohan (1998) versions. From matching plaids to matching suits, both girls have wardrobes I envied when I was younger. Peter Pan collars and twirly dresses . . . oh my.

The Sound of Music (1965) Liesl's dresses are darling, little Gretl's dirndls too cute, and their matching play clothes made from the drapes? Enviable.

Gidget (1959) Gidget is a girl after my own heart; a tenacious little thing played in various films in the series by a young brunette Sally Field or a young blonde Sandra Dee. Regardless of her hair color, Gidget has all the charisma and charm a girl could want. And the most charming wardrobe of vintage beach fashions a girl could want, too.

What a Way to Go (1964) Edith Head costumes galore! Feast your eyes on this raucous ride of a Shirley MacLaine comedy. Gowns, gowns, and more gowns, and furs from the bedroom to the red carpet. Towards the end of the movie Louisa (Shirley MacLaine) comes out in hands-down the most stunning black bikini I've ever seen in my life, a vision against an entirely pink house. Then she gets out of a pink car wearing head-to-toe pink, with pink hair, pink lipstick, pink jewels, and a floor-length pink chinchilla coat. Though she is sad, it's one of the most delightful sights.

All through high school I wore a small rotation of sweatshirts and jeans. My favorites (dorking-out for a second) were my speech team sweatshirt and a blue fleece zip-up from a golf resort in Minnesota. Yes, yes, I was on speech team. Since it was *almost* my only extracurricular activity (sigh, I have to admit I was also in Latin Club), it was the only opportunity I had to have a shirt with my name on it. I wore my speech team sweatshirt with my last name on it far more proudly than I should have.

The winter version of sweatshirt-and-shorts is what I call my "writer outfit": sweatshirt and sweatpants. If it's a boyfriend/husband sweatshirt, that's even better. Tip: Steal two so while one is being "re-appropriated" with his scent, you can wear the other one, then trade off.

I find it hilarious that the styles of what I call "cozy pants," and the fancy world calls "lounge pants," and pretty much everyone else calls "sweats," (ew, no one wants the sweats) change over the years. My mom wore stirrup leggings and legwarmers when she was my age. Then it was oversized straight sweatpants with no band at the bottom. Then it was yoga pants. Then leggings. We're still on leggings, with a new option: the Jogger. They are sweatpants mixed with leggings mixed with . . . jogging pants, perhaps? I'm not one for jogging so I'm not sure. But I approve. My problem with the open-leg sweatpants phase was that when in bed they rode up your leg, leaving you cold and with uncomfortably bunched-up pants. You might as well be wearing shorts. The jogger, which is loose at the hip and thigh, straight on the rest of the leg, and ends in a tight band, is ideal. I was introduced to joggers at a very fancy boutique a few years ago where I spent way too much money for a pair that was already (intentionally) threadbare. I dare not tell you how much I spent, or what has happened to the already-threadbare-when-I-bought-it butt of these pants. Now you can grab a pair at Target or Old Navy and they're probably thicker and a heck of a lot cheaper, so grab two pairs (Ok, honestly? Like five, or maybe seven so you have one for each day of the week). Then buy yourself a Starbucks drink and get a manicure and you're close to what I spent on those first joggers.

Speaking of clothes I've spent too much money on, let me tell you about a favorite vintage find. My vintage Dartmouth College varsity sweater is one of my prized possessions. The Dartmouth "D" varsity sweater is a long-standing tradition, but now they simply stick on a "D" patch and call it a day. Back in the 1960s and prior, local knitting companies made the sweaters with knitted-in Ds and a whole lot of vintage charm. My favorite coffee shop in Hanover, NH, where Dartmouth is, had a clothing shop attached. I find myself drawn to coffee shops that have thrift shops attached—how could I not? This shop somehow tracked down a collection of various vintage varsity sweaters, and had them displayed in the front windows. Now, a financially-struggling grad student meeting her professor for coffee (that he paid for, thank goodness) is in no frame of mind to be making purchasing decisions. But this sweater. *This sweater.* It was too darling. I just imagined a little 1960s bouncy college co-ed wearing it with a plaid skirt and I couldn't get over it. I wanted to be that girl. I tried the sweater on. It fit like a dream. The saleslady told me I looked like a "cute old-school Dartmouth cheerleader" and those words were magic. I plunked down (ahemcan'ttellyouitwastoomuch) for the sweater and now indulge my 1960s Dartmouth cheerleader fantasies during the winter for Dartmouth's traditional Winter Carnival and Homecoming.

I have far too many workout clothes for how often I actually work out. Far too many bathing suits for how often I actually go swimming (I live in Vermont, let's be real). And far too many tennis skirts for how often I actually play tennis. I tend to be a poser when it comes to athletic pursuits, and if I'm going to pose, I like to look good doing it. Besides, tennis skirts and knee highs are obviously the best part of tennis. Anyway, my big problem with workout clothes is the tummy roll. I have a tummy roll, and pretty much every synthetic workout shirt I own finds that tummy roll and well . . . rolls up it. Do you know what I mean? These days I prefer to wear a colorful sports bra with a loose cotton tank over the top. A girl can wear pretty much anything to slackline, one of my favorite athletic pursuits, but I prefer eighties style apparel for the heck of it. Or pretty dresses. I've been a dancer my entire life, and occasionally rotate in my chiffon skirts, leotards, legwarmers, and warm-up tops.

Slackline 101

A slackline is similar to a tight rope except that it is . . . well, a slack line. Slack because it is a looser tension to give it bounce, and a line because it is flat webbing. Developed by climbers using their climbing gear, particularly by a teenager in the 1970s, slacklining and its variants (highlining, tricklining, yoga slacking, etc.) are fast-growing sports in and of themselves as well as useful cross-training for various disciplines. You can purchase an easy-to-set-up slackline ready to go or you can make your own using climbing webbing and gear. You'll want to protect any trees you're using to support your slackline, whether you are slacking in a park for an hour, or leaving it up in your backyard for weeks. A 1-inch line is preferred, though some people use 2-inch webbing. I personally prefer 1-inch webbing, as it is easier to find your balance point. Getting up on the slackline will probably be your biggest hurdle. Knees start to shake uncontrollably when faced with the prospect. Push into your leg on the line and commit, hopping up and grounding yourself fully with that one foot. Then put the other one on the line. Keep your knees slightly bent, your chest slightly forward, and your hands above your head. The hand motions while slacklining are very monkey-like as you swing them back and forth overhead to balance. Practice standing still, walking, and eventually bouncing. Focus on the tree or anchor point and don't forget to breathe. You'll find every muscle in your body and every cell in your brain engages. This is the beauty of slacklining.

Going to the Ballet or the Opera (or a "Fancy Work Thing")

Because you do that, right? I do. Ever since I was little, I've adored the ballet, and my parents took me and my brother to the symphony with season passes. For my eighteenth birthday, I asked for opera tickets. My parents bought us opening night tickets, and because opening night is black tie, this was particularly exciting. My dad rented a tuxedo, and I wore a magnificent vintage fuchsia satin gown and opera-length gloves that made me feel like Jackie Kennedy in the White House years. My dad may have listened to his iPod the entire time, but I soaked up every detail of the glamorous world. Dressing up for a night at a gala event is the frosting of life, the glittering constellation of excitement, art, and the downright sensual allure of being fancy.

Even though I spent most of my high-school days showing off my dorkiness, I also collected vintage dresses. I had a few Victor Costas I loved, and a high number of black velvet cocktail dresses. My favorite to collect was Pucci, which, of course, even in those days was impossibly hard to find. But I managed to find a Pucci dress for $1, and a Pucci robe for a few. These are two thrifting highs, of course. Not all of my fancy dresses were thrifted. I loved shopping at high-end stores such as Saks Fifth Avenue and found a Tadashi gown on clearance that I had to have. We call it my "car wash" dress because the top was a simple crew-neck, but the waist to the floor was a fanciful riot of very-thick strips of fringe. When you moved, you looked like an old-fashioned car wash. I wore it to work at a gala for a film festival I was helping with, and was quite tickled pink as a seventeen-year-old to find one of the ritzy ladies attending was wearing the very same dress. (Funny story there—the event was held at the Ritz Carlton, and I was coming to the venue from another festival event. I was dressing and doing my hair and makeup in the Ritz bathroom when I dropped a contact on the floor. My goodness you guys, I could have died. With only a second's hesitation, I popped it right back in my eye. I'm not kidding when I say that Ritz bathroom was cleaner than my own at home, and I figured the 5-second rules applies to things you're putting in your eyes, too, right? I don't have any eye infections yet, fingers crossed, more than a decade later.)

Collecting Pucci

Italian designer Emilio Pucci is my hands-down favorite. He start-ed selling his designs in the 1950s, and they were trend-setting, wave-making graphic patterns in revolutionary stretch fabrics. He is often called "The Prince of Prints" and his name, "Emilio," is always hidden within his signature bold designs. Pucci is unique in that his fashion empire extended to hosiery, ties, lingerie, towels, and more. I have a few Pucci pillowcases, many scarves, and a robe. I would love to find vintage Pucci tights or panties (they're so cute, I die). But Pucci is not only my favorite; he is an eternal favorite of fashion and vintage lovers alike and his pieces generally go for hundreds of dollars. These are rare finds. Of course, one needn't hunt and peck for Pucci, since the house is still producing gorgeous items, if you can afford the price tag.

New Designer Favorite: Katie Ermilio

Katie Ermilio's grandfather was Grace Kelly's personal clothier. These days, Katie's own clothing line shows sophistication wise beyond her years, a throw-back to an era of glamorous proportions and riotous color. Strapless silk playsuit, anyone? Yes please.

This is a good twirling dress, I declare

And no one is too old for a twirl or a dramatic entrance

On a sweeping set of stairs, like Princess Grace or Coco Chanel

We are women who find beauty in the way a dress drapes

In the way a handbag nestles in the crook of our arms

We are women who do not shy away from

Long marble hallways and high heels

I wear twirling dresses to the post office

And to the thrift store where I hope to stumble across

Gold-tinged champagne flutes and perhaps an antique

Book with golden-edged pages or a globe with countries

To dream of visiting to haul back treasures with memories attached

Like barnacles to my sail-around-the-world houseboat

Do not be afraid to feel beautiful

Because confidence is found there

Do not hesitate to need love, darlings

Because strength is found there

Do not hesitate to dress yourselves with verve

And joie de vivre, for this is the stuff that

Chance and silver linings live for

When we look in mirrors I hope we see women

Who live in light and walk on air and don't care

About the number someone called a size but rather the number

Of smiles we can fit in a day and the breadth of our hearts

Wrapped in the fabric of hope

Hemlines do not define our worth

And the name on the label is no one I know

I would much rather hear the name of the woman who wears

The twirling dress with confidence

Who speaks of knowing she is worthy.

• • • • • • • • • • • • • •

Anyway, we're talking about fashion . . . I have nothing against a thigh-high slit or a to-there back on special occasions. The visual balance is the key. Don't combine a thigh-high slit and a to-there back in one dress. Show off one feature, and show it off good, girl. The same goes for hair and makeup or the dress; choose one to accentuate. Having full-on hair and makeup in addition to a visually busy dress is costume-y and overdone. A busy dress invites simple hair and makeup, and vice-versa.

Consider a high-end dress for a high-end occasion. You will feel like a princess. A high-end dress will make you feel more confident because it will fit better and skim the body in a luxurious way. Chances are you can snag a gorgeous designer gown at a local consignment store for a fraction of the new price, and you can re-consign it. Or nowadays, go the easy route and rent a dress online. If you are wearing an inexpensive fabric, go with black. Cheaper fabrics don't take dyes well and light colors will show off the imperfections of the fabric instead of highlighting the perfections of you. Regardless of the price tag, spend the time and money to get your dress tailored. This eliminates any flaws of the dress and flatters every curve of you. Tailoring is some of the best money you can spend for an event, even on an inexpensive dress.

When it comes to formal wear, the shoes, handbag, and coat are all as important as the dress. If one is off, the entire ensemble falls flat. You want to be a diamond in a platinum setting, not a cubic zirconium in a platinum setting, or worse yet, a diamond in a sterling silver setting. A proper evening coat cannot be underestimated. This is a fancy coat, made of fur, faux fur, velvet, silk, or a lovely wool. No puffy down coats, for Pete's sake. It should slink off you and match the level of sophistication of your dress. I love a coat check, and most fancy events will have one. Tip the attendant when you pick up your coat. Shoes, of course, should be fancy-fancy and can even out-fancy the dress. If in doubt, go for neutral gold or silver that matches your jewelry. Remember, the fancier the dress, the higher the heel should be, as long as you can manage it. If you can't walk in heels, a lower heel is better than a wobbly high one. Let me tell you a secret: the really expensive shoes are actually truly comfortable, and there's a reason stars can wear them all night and to the after-party. Investing in good shoes is never a mistake.

A handbag for evening should almost always be an actual handbag or clutch. If it does have a shoulder strap, it simply must be a high quality one.

Otherwise, keep your bag in your hand or tucked under an arm as you mingle, and in your lap as you dine. No handbags on the table, even fancy ones such as Judith Lieber bags that are truly art. Gloves are rarely worn these days, but you may generally wear them all day and evening, even while drinking, shaking hands, and dancing, until you are seated for dinner. Keep your gloves in your lap or clutch as soon as you're seated and while eating. If a hat or fascinator is worn, make sure you are confident and comfortable enough to wear it all evening. A fascinator (a trend I sincerely hope is catching on in America these days) is generally tipped over the right eye and worn on the side that has less hair when parted (see page 150 for more details). A lady never need remove her hat indoors, though of course, please be polite if wearing a hat at the theatre or opera and do not obstruct anyone's view.

That Workaday Grind

For Monday through Friday, life needs to be easy, right? We're running out the door, and if you're like me, coffee takes a bit more precedence than style most days. I find a weekly uniform works wonders. If you build a wardrobe in a *parrot* *plum* coordinated color palette, getting dressed is easy. Grab one piece from each category and it should all meld into one marvelous outfit. I love color, though, so my palette is a hearty mix *peach* of colors and neutrals that can all be tied together with the right scarf in winter or handbag in summer. If you have a casual office or work from home or a studio like me, I love these uniforms:

Dark skinny jeans + tee shirt + long (bottom-covering) vest (or replace the tee shirt and vest with a tunic) + scarf + ankle booties or funky flats
Dark high-waist trouser jeans + printed or plain silk blouse tucked in + great leather belt + chunky bracelets + ankle booties or funky flats

If you're in an office where things need to be a bit more professional, here are your go-tos:

Pencil skirt + tee shirt + amazing necklace + funky shoes

Wool suit pants + printed or plain silk blouse tucked in + a long elegant pendant necklace + a great suit jacket + embellished low heels

Of course when I say tee shirt I'm not talking about your husband's ratty alma mater crew neck. We're grown-ups, or at least trying to be during the week. A loose-fitting cotton-and-modal blend will do wonders for your wardrobe. They're stretchy and soft, and the modal makes them last longer in the wash. Go for the neckline that works best with your body, then buy a selection: pocket tees, embellished necklines, the entire color spectrum, various sleeve lengths, various lengths in general, and various textures. This should be a large section in your wardrobe because chances are you'll wear one every day.

Most offices will want closed-toe shoes, which is why I suggest ankle booties or funky flats. In Vermont, Birkenstocks are totally appropriate office-wear in most offices, but that's neither here nor there (though I do love me some Birkenstocks, I admit). Experiment with various cuffs on your skinny jeans to show off the shoes in summer. I love a Mary Jane with an almond toe these days, and metallic shoes are in and can be a fun way to play up your office outfits. I'm not giving up my leopard-print smoking slippers anytime soon, nor my dalmation-print pony-hair flats. These make an outfit.

While I work from my studio most days, I do love when I need to get dressed up for a meeting and can pull out one of my pencil skirts (it's that modern-vintage vibe, you know?). I have them in all textures . . . wide-whale corduroy, a fabulous thick herringbone wool, a nude faux-leather. I used to have a white leather one that was so fun to dress up, but alas, it is no longer. A tee shirt keeps things casual and is layer-able, which is important in an office environment. For something a bit fancier, go for a printed or plain silk blouse. Keep that sweater or blazer close at hand for when they crank the AC or you have to dash out of the office for a quick meeting. An amazing necklace ties the whole thing together. Shoes are your fun factor. When the rest of your outfit is professional, you can get away with funkier shoes. But let me tell you a secret: Nothing makes a pencil skirt mumsy faster than flats. It's just a fact of nature, I'm afraid. Because of this fact, I'm a big fan of wedges in the office because they are sturdy and easy to walk in. Ain't nobody got time for stilettos 9-to-5, much as I love a fancy shoe. A confident gait is more important than sky-high shoes that have you wincing by lunchtime.

The Power of a White Tee Shirt and Jeans

Oh, the beauty of simplicity! A good white tee shirt and good jeans can take you just about anywhere. The key? Proper fit. This doesn't mean that every piece needs to be slim-fitting, but rather that the drape should always be attractive and soft, showing off what should be shown off on a woman. This may be a Hanes V-neck or it may be a $90 Splendid tee. I have both in my wardrobe. A Hanes V-neck can be insanely attractive with a pair of jeans, casually tucked into the waistband on one end, worn with a high ponytail and knock-out sunglasses. I find it funny but true that a white tee shirt and jeans, in pretty much any variation, will always be a hit with the men. It is a can't-fail first-date outfit; I think even more failproof than a sundress.

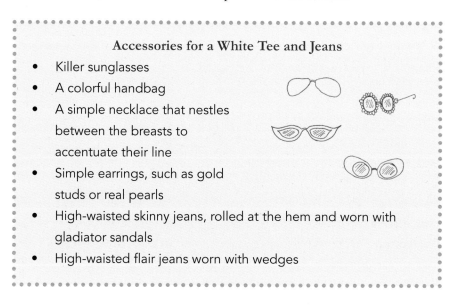

Accessories for a White Tee and Jeans

- Killer sunglasses
- A colorful handbag
- A simple necklace that nestles between the breasts to accentuate their line
- Simple earrings, such as gold studs or real pearls
- High-waisted skinny jeans, rolled at the hem and worn with gladiator sandals
- High-waisted flair jeans worn with wedges

- Straw sunhat or fedora
- Big beach bag
- Fancy clutch and fancy jewelry
- Eyeglasses and bedhead
- A high ponytail under a baseball cap and lip gloss
- A silk scarf around your neck or in your hair
- A big fancy camera around your neck
- Fancy undies just for you

Guide to Shopping Vintage

Fit, Quality, Cleanliness, Uniqueness, Price

These are the things you want to think about when you're shopping vintage. If you find something high quality and totally unique that fits perfectly and is in your price range, you've struck vintage gold. But most often, the arm holes are too high, the bust too pointy, the waist too tiny, the cleanliness not up to par, and the price . . . well, even the most dreamy gem will break a girl's heart with that last one.

Fit: This one is up for debate. Purists think you should never alter vintage, but many vintage pieces simply do not fit the bodies of today's women (or the bras, to be honest). I have only altered one vintage dress because it needed some TLC anyway. I think it's much more fun to find that a vintage piece fits like a glove and seems like it was made for you. A good seamstress can, however, make a few adjustments that will make wearing vintage more comfortable: they can lower armholes (I don't know why vintage armholes seems to be on the neck practically), lower the bust, and adjust the waist and hemline. But if you can't zip it, my darling, walk away, hard as it may be.

Quality: I cannot stress this enough: just because it's vintage doesn't make it quality. Some materials back in the day are not worth reprising, in my opinion. However, many items were made with fabulous fabrics in a quality we can't find these days. Look for 100% cotton, real silk, 100% wool, and I don't even mind some seventies shiny polyester in the right context (dance the night away, disco girl).

Cleanliness: Vintage means old, there's no getting around that. It is part of the charm, but not-so-much when it is tattered and of dubious cleanliness. Check the zipper and make sure it's in good shape (though a seamstress can replace this), make sure any netting or tulle isn't full of holes, make sure the armpits aren't stained to death (trust me, this comes alive again when worn), the scent is something you can tolerate, and the fabric won't have you itching constantly. When it comes to cleaning vintage, there are a few tricks you can keep up your sleeve (see page 88), but the cleaner to begin with, the better.

Uniqueness: Again, just because it's vintage doesn't make it cool. There are plenty of seventies country-style maxi dresses I wouldn't be caught dead in. (Though I have a green polyester one that makes me feel divine.) But uniqueness does play a big factor in why we love vintage. No one else will be walking down the street wearing your dress. The more unique the piece, the better. I went through a phase of collecting vintage cardigans before I realized they were pretty much all exactly the same and so similar to today's styles you couldn't tell the difference. I weeded through the collection and only kept the most unique pieces. Cashmere with a little Peter Pan collar and pink embroidered flowers? Yes, please.

Price: I hate to say it, but vintage clothing in great shape can be very pricey and sometimes more expensive than new things. If the above factors are in order, the piece warrants a higher price. I love my local vintage clothing store's $10 "Needs TLC" bin, because I can do minor repairs for that price. For me, the thrill of the hunt factors in, and finding a great vintage piece in an unlikely place (say, a church garage sale) makes it all the better. But a vintage clothing store filled with frilly concoctions and new-old-stock pieces is heaven, too—just be prepared to pay more.

My Favorite Things to Find Vintage

- Wool "secretary" dresses with girly details
- Vintage sundresses (very wearable in cotton)
- Unbeatable hats of all kinds
- 1950s swimsuits
- Margaret Smith handbags
- Barkcloth maxi dresses from the late sixties
- Swimsuit cover-ups, playsuits, and loungewear
- Vintage evening clutches
- Fur pieces, such as hats, trimmed scarves/coats/sweaters, collars, earmuffs, and caplets

Keeping Your Vintage in Good Shape

I've picked up a few tricks here and there for caring for vintage clothing. One of my favorite tricks for anything vintage and/or delicate is to put it in a Ziploc bag and stick it in the freezer for 2 weeks. I'm being serious. My freezer is often chock-full of Ziploc bags of vintage hats and clutches along with dinner fixings. This is scientifically proven to be almost as effective as any other cleaning method at killing germs and bugs. While it won't take out stains, this is my favorite way to refresh vintage pieces, especially pieces that can't be cleaned any other way. For things that can take water, you'll want to hand-wash rather than taking things to the dry cleaners (Oh I've had so many pieces ruined by the dry cleaner I can't even tell you; I stopped going entirely once they ruined a St. John sweater). I love to hand wash my vintage and delicate pieces. Just be sure to use a very, very delicate soap as many can leave residues that will damage the fibers. Use only cold water! Do not wring pieces, and swish very gently. Don't let them soak too long as this can relax the fibers too much. Vintage dyes don't always hold well, but don't worry, just carry on quickly and let the pieces dry thoroughly on like-colored towels before wearing.

For drying, put out a plush towel on the floor, gently place the item on it, and re-stretch to original shape. Then roll the towel up and give it a gentle squeeze to get as much water out as possible. Vintage clothing tends to be very heavy or very delicate, so it's best to dry it on a fresh towel lying flat. But vintage sundresses and nighties look especially cheerful flying on a clothesline. For white cottons (not wool or silk), lying flat in the sunshine will bring extra life back to them as the sun naturally and gently bleaches. Hats can be steamed and brushed to bring life back to them, and the same is true of coats. I never recommend using mothballs as the scent is entirely overwhelming, but you'll want to be sure to keep cedar blocks or balls in your vintage collection to keep moths at bay. They find vintage clothing as yummy as we do, unfortunately. If you have an item that simply can't be put in the freezer or hand washed, such as a coat, I recommend Dryel, the at-home dry cleaning system you use in your dryer.

Lingerie

Oh, I love pretty lingerie! It makes my day. I love opening my underwear drawer and seeing colorful frilly things. I love matching my underthings to my outfit for a simple sense of satisfaction for the day. At least I've got one thing together, dang it, even if it's my underwear! I also like letting a boyfriend pick out my underthings to give us both a secret smile. I've really enjoyed going high-quality with my underwear. This has made such a huge difference in my life, truly. I feel like a grown-up with HankyPanky or OnGossamer underwear—real lingerie brands, instead of bulk-packaged underwear. A properly fitting bra will do wonders for your self-esteem too. I highly recommend going to a real lingerie shop or high-end department store and getting a professional bra fitting. I always thought I didn't "measure up" to a certain bra size I was used to wearing. Turns out I needed to go up a cup size or two depending on the bra, but needed to go down in band size. This created a drastic difference in the shape of my body (va-va-voom) and my confidence, as the bra looked

great and sat perfectly on my now-perky "cupcakes" (as I call my breasts). Not going to lie, that makes a girl feel good, right?

I like to keep my lingerie drawer organized. Clear plastic underwear organizers are standard at any home store, and they make a world of difference. I have two for socks and two for underwear. My underwear are divided into neutrals and colors. In between the socks and underwear is an open space to keep bras flat, not folded cup-into-cup, but nested into each other. This makes things easy to find and easily rotated. It's now a little morning joy instead of fumbling through a mess of tangled undergarments first thing.

When it comes to pajamas, I'm once again split on my pleasures. In winter it's all about leggings and a sweatshirt. Leggings with tall socks on top keep me warmest (remember, I live in Vermont). In the summer, I wear my floaty collection of vintage nighties. I call them "Grandma Nighties" but really they were worn by my grandma when she was my age (not these exact ones, obviously), which is endearing. They are all chiffon-dreamy, lace-frilled, and watercolor-cute. I adore them and keep them hanging from a hook in my room so I can admire their frothiness.

Here's another secret: the simple pleasure of a garter belt and thigh-high stockings is quite unparalleled. This contraption is confusing to many and has largely been relegated to the bedroom for sexy time, but take it into the fancy world and give it a whirl. Granted, you'll need some high-quality (Wolford or Fogal) stay-up stockings that actually stay put to make this indulgence enjoyable. Just remember: You wear your garter under your underwear (if you're wearing any #justsayin).

Makeup

I only have 2 makeup "secrets" to tell you: do your brows every. single. day. regardless of whether you'll be going out of the house or not, and if you only have time for one extra touch, do lipstick or lip gloss. When I say "do your brows" I mean brush them into place with a spoolie and fill them in if necessary with a like-colored powder and a brush. And here are some not-so-much-secrets: Drink lots of water, get good sleep, sweat out toxins, eat a balanced diet, and moisturize, moisturize, moisturize. Everything else is basically technique.

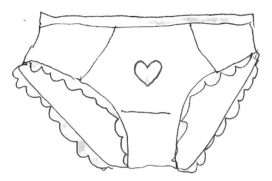

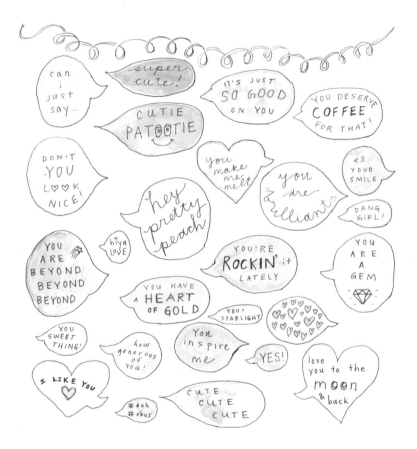

Community

"THE HIGH LUXURY OF NOT HAVING TO EXPLAIN . . ." —VIRGINIA WOOLF

How to Make Friends as an Adult

Oh, it can be a tricky thing to make new friends as an adult. I often find myself awkwardly spouting out, "I want to be your friend!"—which is not my smoothest move. If the person is also caffeine crazy, it might work out. If not, well, I'm just the spazzball who wants to hug a stranger right now.

Generally, friends are made from common interests, be they hobbies or circumstances you happen to find yourselves in. I'm not going to lie, this feels much like dating. I know, I know, it's uncomfortable. This is why going to events and finding friends on common ground is important. It is hard to find friends when you're at home in your pajamas. Put yourself in situations where you'll find like-minded people . . . book signings, concerts, the law library, business networking events, wherever you think your people might be. This narrows the potential friend-field to people you're more likely to get along with.

A lot of times we find our "first week of school friends" before we eventually settle into our group, which may or may not include the first week of school friends. You know what I mean? The ones you sort of cling to desperately before lunchtime so you have someone to sit with and you can look for them the rest of the first week. By then, you might have met other people in classes that invite you to eat lunch with them. I find this an important tactic

93

for anything in life, really: find your first week at school friends. At a conference, find your "first 10 minutes at the conference" friends. Find your "here we are waiting for this 10-hour delayed plane" friends. Find your "we're all here at this awkward work event together" friends. Who knows, they may stick around for a long time, or you may find others you click with better.

What do you say to a potential friend? You say, "Hi, I'm Natalie!" and you say it with the exclamation point in your voice. Except use your name, not mine. Use that friendly little lilt that tips the word up at the end and sounds inviting and, well, friendly. Then they'll say their name. This is where things get tricky. Don't let the conversation stall out here, or you'll be forced to make up a lame excuse to get another drink even though yours is still full or to answer a non-ringing phone. Keep the conversation flowing. Find something to say. Anything. Ok, not *anything*. What you're looking for is a transition from your introduction to other benign-but-slightly-more-interesting-and-personal topics. Here are some Natalie-approved small talk topics:

The weather: This is a stand-by topic and I still stand by it. People love to talk about the weather, and there are so many ways it can segue into a different conversation. There's almost always something unusual to discuss in the weather. "Gorgeous fall we've had, right?" can turn into, "Yes, in fact, I was just rock climbing and my, the foliage was excellent," or, "I just drove up north and stayed at this great little B&B, have you heard of it?" and boom, you've got a conversation topic.

Careers: Your respective careers are a great starting place for a conversation. In fact, it's one of the most basic building blocks of speech, "What do you do?" Instant springboard.

A recent movie or book: Again, an easy topic to turn into a conversation. Just make sure the movie or book you choose to mention is appropriate for the audience. I like to imagine you're all watching indie hits and under-the-radar foreign films, but the  latest blockbuster trilogy-based-on-book is probably more likely to garner a good response. "Hey, have you seen the new [latest hit]?" and if you're lucky, your respondent will say, "Oh my goodness yes, it was *so good!*" or "No, I haven't, have you?! Is it worth seeing?!" with as much enthusiasm as my punctuation implies.

A good magazine article you read: Also acceptable would be a *credible* internet article from a website that you can *remember*. No one likes that, "Oh I read somewhere this thing about, wait, where did I see that? Aunt Shirley's Facebook, maaaaybe? Did I even click through or did I just read the headline? But anyway it was suuuuuuper interesting." Great story. Don't be that person, okay? An interesting magazine article to discuss needn't be all highfalutin' and intellectual, either. If it comes from, say, *Architectural Digest* and is an article about which top-of-the-line appliances celebrities have, bring it up. "Have you heard about the new Actenk dishwasher series out of Denmark? All the celebrities have them now, I guess they're thousands of dollars!" then you can either celebrity gossip or talk interior design, depending on where your companion takes the conversation. (Side note: love me some celebrity gossip now and again, just sayin'.)

A place you just traveled or are going to travel to: Travel can be a sensitive subject, so approach with humility and a bit of tourist excitement to be well-received. A trip you're taking soon is a great conversation topic because you can ask for suggestions on things to do. But no one likes the boaster who climbed Machu Picchu barefoot, backwards, and alone. Keep things light and tell a funny story about getting carsick in the bus (nope, scratch that, throw-up stories are never polite) or getting mistaken for a celebrity.

I usually stay away from: sports (not everyone follows and it can cause heated debates, especially here in New England), religion/politics/sex/any hot button issue (I mean, I'm not sure why any of these would come up in the first conversation with someone, but avoid if possible), your own accomplishments at great length, or anything that requires jargon and special knowledge.

A good rule of thumb when engaging in small talk is to go with the improv comedy principle of saying, "Yes, *and.*" This is a way of training your brain to not shut the door in a conversation. It also doesn't embarrass your comedy/conversational partner. A "no" in polite conversation is, well, impolite, and often a dead stop.

Being me, I like to jump right into deep philosophical topics, such as the state of arts and culture in our generation. You have to read the crowd for this to work, though, or you might get singled out as the weird-writer-girl. Maybe that's just me, but really, read the crowd. Some, likely fellow artists, will welcome the chance to slide below the surface of polite conversation into deeper waters. Just be careful, as this may cause someone to fall in love with you*.

When Friends Aren't Friends Anymore

Buffering the lives of others is emotionally draining. Be on the lookout for those people who erase your margin and take a disproportionate amount of energy for what they give. Of course, we all go through phases in life where we need more support from our friends, but that is different from a consistent energy drain.

---

* There's just something about diving beneath the surface right off the board that makes someone irresistibly attractive. Don't say I didn't warn you.

It's a tough lesson to learn, but try to only keep relationships where you are on the same plane of reciprocity. I am not suggesting score-keeping by any means, only an equal investment in the relationship. Take stock of your relationships. Are they two-way, or a little lopsided? Are you constantly chasing someone down, constantly doing favors for them, or only wanted when it is convenient for them? These relationships are not healthy and erode self-confidence quickly. It is easy to get trapped in the neediness of such relationships, which I wholeheartedly understand. As much as we are wired to be self-involved, it seems we are equally wired to be needed. Being needed feels good. Until it doesn't, you know what I mean? It's "No problem!" the first time they ask for a favor, but each successive time, particularly without any offer of gratitude, it becomes more and more of a problem.

friends?

☐ yes

☐ no

How do you extricate yourself gracefully from this sort of relationship without burning the bridge? Well, you can try, but the bridge may get burned, or at least scorched, in the process. And I think that's generally okay. I am standing up for you! No one gets to take advantage of you without going through me first. Courtesy and kindness are still appropriate, though, so there will be no silent treatment, blocking of calls, or avoidance scenarios. We are adults here, and we'll confront the problem head-on.

"I'm so sorry, but I won't be able to cat-sit/airport-run/lend-you-money/ bail-you-out-of-jail *[that thing you're always asking me to do]* anymore." That should be enough, but you may need to follow up with, "It's simply too overwhelming for me." Or "I'm afraid I'm cat-sat/airport-run/money-lent/bail-you-out-ed out." These put the onus on you and help soften the blow. It's hard to take offense when someone says they're overwhelmed in life. And of course it is the truth.

We occasionally have to break up with friends. This is not easy and is very similar to a romantic break-up. It is worth it, though, to break up with friends who are toxic or who take-take-take. The best way to break up with a friend is directly, to avoid any confusion. A simple, "I'm so sorry, but I just don't think we can be friends right now," should get the point across gently.

Strangers

I love a good stranger. Wait, that sounds weird . . . what I mean is, I like it when people are good strangers to other strangers. Strangers become allies, perhaps the only people who will ever share a specific moment with us, and often strangers become life-long friends. Such a mysterious thing, being strangers. Staying strangers. Being once-strangers-now-friends. Being once-strangers-now-lovers. Then add in, once-strangers-then-lovers-now-strangers-again. But no matter, I'm getting off track. I love when strangers, particularly in airports or in other stressful situations, offer a helping hand or a genuine smile.

I am a big fan of the compliment. I never let a good compliment go unsaid. I will track people down to tell them I like their shoes/scarf/hair/color they're wearing/smile/glasses. Only because I believe people should be applauded and told they are beautiful. I have done this since I was tiny, telling strangers I liked their lipstick or earrings. I like to appreciate the little things people bring into the world, even when they are as small as a beautiful scarf that piques my curiosity. Compliments are the stuff of poetry, too. I can't tell you how many times a comment from a stranger has inspired a line or even an entire poem. It's like giving a free gift. What does it take from me to tell someone I like what they're wearing? Nothing, it is free. It is free if my heart is free, and gives it without strings attached.

• • • • • • • • • • • • • •

I am a perpetual student of the inner workings of

This great and beautiful machine called

Life

But I tend to call it "Bravery and Responsibility"
Or "Joy in Orderliness"
As if every word I speak is a thesis statement
And I aim to make my living the dissertation

My glasses may not be rose-colored
But when I push them up on my nose
I squint to make my dimples show and I tap
The pencil against the side of my head because
I see glass doorknobs when I look at the stars
With my two hands I reach out to open as many as I can
To find their secrets and to ponder why on earth
Or in heaven
The galaxies are so vast and glorious

I will read and write great words
And dig through numbers and charts and graphs
Looking for veins of gold
I gather pennies on my walk to the forum of knowledge
Where I declare that love is the only thing we can give
Without strings attached
And by the way when did we stop doing that?

While the others were on a fool's errand

I will find that the world has shifted

On its axis and they hadn't noticed

I will notice, with strong spirit and steady heart

I will keep it afloat and hoist it on my shoulders, then

And lift my voice

"Come, darlings, let's fix this ailing planet of ours,

Bring coffee, quickly, and the crossword puzzle."

• • • • • • • • • • • • •

I love holding doors, buying coffee for strangers in line behind me, telling out-of-towners how to use the parking ticket machine. And I love when good strangers help me put my suitcase in the overhead bin, offer me the last box of gluten-free cookies when we both reach for them, or help me when my car is smoking at the rest area and offer to follow me to the closest auto repair shop . . . we are all doing life together. People amaze me. Good strangers delight me.

Being a good stranger involves risk. It involves putting yourself out there. Outside of your comfort zone and personal space. Being a good stranger means paying attention to the world around you and being attentive to the needs of others that you might be witnessing. Being a good stranger doesn't always end well, I admit. But I won't let that stop me from living life here on this planet with two hands willing to help, quick to offer, and free for the taking.

Cultivating Friends of All Ages

I relish having friends of all ages. It is so enriching to have friends both older and younger than you. Peers are great, and necessary, but I love having friends at different stages of life. They are gifts to me. They remind me that life is fleeting, youth is wondrous, and age is well-earned.

Parents of a friend who has moved away have become cherished friends of mine, and the three of us enjoy a familial dinner once a month. Maybe twice a year my friend is home and joins us, but otherwise his parents and I text, drop by, give each other gifts, and cheer each other on. Another friend who worked with me at a gift shop is my mom's age, but doesn't have children of her own. She saves the fashion section of the *Wall Street Journal* and her Clinique makeup samples for me. I have a friend I call my "Internet Momma" and we live in different states and have never met, but we pray for each other, text, call, send cards. A friend at church has the same birthday as me (but a few decades difference), and I bring her a birthday crown each year and she shows me scarves and hats she bought because they remind her of me.

Friends who are younger than me serve another role in my life. I mean a few years younger than me all the way down to five-year-olds who invite me to their birthday parties and give me unicorn Valentines. Granted, I'm usually friends with the parents of the young ones as well, but you wouldn't know it when I go over to their houses and get pounced on by the kids. I might say hello to their parents fifteen minutes later when I emerge from Lego- or Barbie-kingdom. I have a seven-year-old gym monkey who follows me around at the climbing gym and we talk like best friends. Rumor has it her dog, Winston, looks adorable when he begs for his dinner with his tongue out, and I believe it.

Kids are so very, very good for the soul. They never cease to amaze me with their curiosity, their imagination, their view of logic and practicality, and the way they live in the moment. Their lack of self-consciousness is endearing and inspiring. My friend's three-year-old little boy is enamored with sprinkles. They light up his world. I have never seen someone so in love with a confectionary topping, but it is infectious. I now have a sprinkle mug and have made sprinkle cookies and sprinkle Rice Krispies treats. He's right, sprinkles make life better.

Being Good Friends

The best kinds of friends are the ones who fold your laundry for you absent-mindedly while you're chatting in the living room. Friends who start making tea the minute you walk through the door without even asking. I love friends who come into my daily life and accept the way it is. Sometimes my apartment is a project-strewn absolute mess and I'm tucked in bed writing like a maniac with half-eaten snacks and piles of used tissues all around me. I hate to say it, but that's how I work a lot. And my real friends have seen that. They've made their own coffee and sat down on the floor by the bed and flipped through the stack of books while I finish writing.

But you have to work up to that. Friends who immediately do that put my defenses up. They haven't earned it. Err on the side of politeness until politeness seems downright hilarious to you both. Then you can let your guard down a bit.

Popping over to a friend's house is an art and a science. In the suburban Midwest, popping over unannounced is common-place. When I moved to New England, I realized that no one does that, ever, end of story. It is also different if friends are single, married, have roommates who come and go, kids that are sleeping at night, and/or tightly packed schedules. Be aware of their priorities and

preferences. These days we're lucky—we can shoot off a text and say, "Hey, I'm out your way, mind if I stop in for a quick chat?" and usually receive an instantaneous response. This courtesy will not go unnoticed.

I never quite get it when friends say, "I can't, I've got to clean up the house today." I say, "I will come help you clean!" If I say it, I mean it. I think it's rather fun, actually, to vacuum together and dance to loud music. This is true with any offer of help . . . if you say you'll help, be ready to pick up the broom, help move the furniture, or mix concrete for their new backyard patio. I am a fan of communal projects when they're fun, but not when they're expected. If I feel something is expected of me, I almost immediately balk and say no. Of course when friends help out like this, a hearty thank-you is a must. They are exchanging their time—in essence, their life—for your benefit. Pizza and coffee are helpful, but they are not enough. Truly sincere words of thankfulness, endless hugs, and a vocal appreciation of your efforts to others are good friend form.

Friendship is also knowing when to back off because friends are not family. They are chosen-family, yes, but there is still not that blood bond and the history of button-pressing, top-blowing, and such that families thrive on. There are family occasions, family memories that we may not be part of, and that's fine. That's the way it should be. I will stand on the side and wait for you to vent to me about Aunt Thelma's terrible cottage-cheese-spinach-strawberry-jello concoction. That's my friend-job. Because friendship is knowing when to be there.

I strive to be a good friend always, but there are times when I mess up and, as a friend says, "lose friendship stars." Of course we don't keep track, but do feel unhappy when our friendship has gone a bit awry. People are people and we disappoint each other. But true friendship brings up the infraction and talks it out, uncomfortable as it may be. True friendship offers olive branches and friendship stars back in abundance.

No One Can Be Everything

This is an important section when it comes to community. No one can be everything. No one can be your everything. Everyone needs a variety of people in their lives. Depending on one person, be it a spouse, best friend, parent, or mentor, causes, well, dependency, and a one-sided view of our lives. Some things we just can't hear from someone close, but someone else makes it hear-able for us. Friends offer different interests, different perspectives, different levels of friendship and support for our lives.

They say it takes a village to raise a child, and I don't think that ever goes away. It takes a village to raise good humans, and to keep them on track their whole lives. Expand your reach if you feel your village is too small. I can usually tell my circle is getting too small when I only have a handful of stories to tell. I prefer to have a bunch of different circles of information and influence so I have plenty of stories to tell in the other circles.

Expecting one person to be your everything is detrimental to both of you. One person can't carry your entire weight, darling. Our lives get heavy and we need to share burdens. People, even the ones we love the most and who love us wholeheartedly, will let us down. It will break their heart, too, even the most big-hearted person in the world, when they accidentally let you down. This can all spiral into depression quite quickly and it ruins friendships, ruins marriages, ruins relationships in general. We are sociable creatures, designed to do life in community. So give your loved ones a break and let them off the hook. They cannot be everything.

And if someone is using you as their everything, help them be healthy by stepping back and offering them the space and grace to expand their circle. I get that it feels good to be needed. It feels good to have someone depend on you. While these are worthwhile things, they cannot be the entirety of the relationship. Give and take space to breathe.

The People in Your Corner

The people in your corner are the deep-circle friends. They're chosen family, or maybe real family. They're your "people." Your emergency contacts, your late-night phone calls, your "same brain" ones. I like to think of it as teamwork. Goodness, having a good team in your corner (is that mixing my metaphors too much?) is half the battle of being successful in life, I think.

Cultivating a team of people takes work. It takes years. It takes attention, enthusiasm, honesty, and vulnerability. Letting people into your life to see your successes and failures is tough. But the good thing about the people in your corner is that once you find them, they're yours forever. They won't leave, at least not easily or willingly. These people, they've signed up. They're wearing the same jersey as you, waving their "YAY YOU!" flags high and shouting loud. And you do it for them. You show up. You come through. You buy their kid's school raffle tickets and a tin of cheese popcorn from the baseball team fundraiser.

Friends like this transcend time and distance. While they may not be able to literally show up as often, they show up by sending flowers, by making time for phone calls, by emailing photos before they show up on social media so that it is a personal connection. It is great when these people are true family, but more often than not, it seems these sorts of people come to us through other avenues, crossing lives with us on some serendipitous path. And we keep traveling with them.

I want to tell you it is okay if these people are not your family. And it's fantastic if they are. I hope they are. Family is one of the greatest gifts in life. But family is family, and we all know what that means. I just want you to know that if your family members aren't necessarily the closest people in your day-to-day life, that's okay. Because it takes a village, remember?

Then there are our balcony people. Oh our balcony people. This is what my dear almost-mother-in-law, Jason's mom, calls those who have gone on before us to Heaven, who are standing on the clouds cheering us on from the balcony of the heavenly realm. We are even more conscious of their missing when we feel successes and they can't celebrate in person with us. But we keep

a seat at the table of our hearts for them. They've helped us get where we are, and for that, we are eternally grateful. I'm blessed to have many in my balcony cheering me on. While I'd much rather hug them here on earth, I look forward to hugging them at the end of the ultimate race, when I reach that balcony, too, and they are still cheering me on.

Adventuring: On Being Brave Again

"WOULD YOU LIKE AN ADVENTURE NOW, OR SHALL
WE HAVE OUR TEA FIRST?" —J.M. BARRIE, FROM PETER PAN

Sometimes life walks you through the park, sits you down on a bench, and says, "Be patient for a while." It is in these quiet, questioning, uncertain times in life we often learn the most about ourselves. We don't always know it at the time, though. Much like sitting on the park bench, you may swing your feet and whistle a bit and feel as if nothing is changing, because you are still sitting. But you have seen sunrises and sunsets. You have watched the way new lovers stroll, the way mothers bend down to nurture children, the glee on the face of dogs out for walks with owners seeking stress relief. You have seen people run to catch buses, walk with heads in books, stroll arm in arm with an elderly parent. You have seen life, taken it in, sifted it, and found that some of what you learned is most worthy of being kept.

But once you've been sitting for a while, there is this strange phenomenon that you must find your center of balance again. Standing up might make you feel quite dizzy as you search for equilibrium. Life can feel extra anxiety-inducing as you try to put the pieces of the old you and the new you together again. Being brave might seem like an impossible task. I have been here. I have stared down the task of starting again, and I have found that with time and diligence, you can be braver in the end than you ever thought possible. Let's get back to brave.

The Big Things

Oftentimes when we're working on getting our brave back, even the smallest tasks seem overwhelming. Staying focused on the big-picture things can help us keep blinders on to distractions from our road to recovery.

Being Good to Yourself: When we're working through a trauma in our lives, our self-care seems to be the first thing that slips. Give yourself grace. You have little extra in your life right now, so saying no to extras is necessary. We are a bit like children in times of trauma. We need some guidance and a bit of discipline and tough love, too. Sometimes we even need to put ourselves in time-out. While we may have dedicated partners who will do this for us, it is our sole responsibility. I have to put myself in a mental time-out every so often to refocus. Avoid acting out as much as you can. I know, I know, trust me I know, how tempting it is. It is our natural inclination. But hold to your basics, focus on healing and on not hiding the pain. We have to expose the pain to air for it to breathe, for it to heal. Resist picking the scabs, tough (and gross) as that is. You know your wound, you know your scabs, and you know what "picking at it" translates to in your situation. Just remember, wounds will itch, sting, and burn as they heal. They will be miserable at times, almost unbearable. But it is part of the process, and it means you are moving forward. Bear up, and be good to yourself.

Watch Out for the Cliff: It's this tricky thing that going a little easy on yourself is necessary but you can't go too easy on yourself. Don't let yourself go too much or too far. There is a cliff, and once you've gone off it you might be stuck down there for good. The only way back up, with terrible toil and trouble, is to go the long way 'round and climb the mountain again. It can be a perilous journey. When you're right on the line, you're going "ripe" as my grandpa calls it. And letting yourself go ripe, or soft, or to look over the cliff and contemplate the jump, is incredibly damaging to your morale and journey back to health. But I will say one good thing for the cliff: it is a warning sign. When you see the cliff, you know you are approaching the point of no return and you can call for help, scramble

to reach safety, put on a harness and a helmet and gather strength to fight for your life. Because this is a fight for your life at this point. There are only two directions: Back to safety or over the cliff. This is no time for those human-flying-squirrel suits or for strapping yourself to a stranger and hoping they pull the parachute cord. No, no, my dear, those are adventures for when you're strong and safe. Now, we must focus on staying strong and safe and getting back to brave. The truth is, going over the cliff is not brave. Going over the cliff is giving up, giving in, and letting yourself go. I don't want you to let go. If you need someone to ask you to stay, here I am, asking you: Won't you please stay? Hold on, hold out, and hold up.

Establish Routine: Routine is important when our brains are overtired. Keeping our lives simple and automatic is important to our sanity. We don't all have someone to hold us to a routine or a standard, but here are things that are easy to routine-ize (totally a word): your food, your clothing, your appointments and commitments, and your basic grooming. For some reason, haircuts, makeup, and grooming tend to go out the window when we're down. This is okay for a short amount of time, but then we'll need to pull it together. It is very hard to see any motivation or light down the road when we're wearing pajamas all day, and the same ones we were wearing yesterday at that. Sometimes we need to look good to feel good. I had a white board on my wall next to my bed that I saw first thing every morning, and I wrote on it, "Get Up, Dress Up, Show Up, Never Give Up." There have been times in my life when I've had to force myself to get out of the house once a day. I'd go to get a coffee and consciously interact with humans.

Focus on Health: Your body is on overload already with stress during any tough time in life, leaving it little extra reserve to fight off viruses or infection. Keep yourself hydrated, well-rested, and well-supplemented with vitamins and minerals that give your body an extra boost. You are your priority. Take time off from work if you need to de-stress. Say no to anything extraneous that drains your limited energy.

Change Your Inner Monologue: A negative inner monologue is one of the biggest hurdles to health. Our minds love to replay negative things and re-hearse worst-case scenarios. This does nothing but drain us of every resource we have. Rehearsing situations, both real and imagined ones, is the most detrimental of inner monologues. It takes your beautiful, curious imagination and uses it to destroy your self-confidence and ability to cope. To change this we have to literally replace our thoughts. We have to mentally quarantine every negative thought like it is a plague that will eat us alive, because, well, it kind of will. Create a standard replacement thought, or a standard image in your head that you instantly switch to the moment a negative thought enters your head. PUPPIES! Beaches! Kitties! "I AM AMAZING!" It has to be happy and encouraging, something that feeds your soul and makes you smile. I'm not going to lie, one of my tricks is to think of my favorite silly words: rubber ducky, fluffer nutter, pumpernickel, and spelunking. These always make me giggle. Another trick? Look up at the sky or ceiling.

For some reason it resets your brain and can help stop negative thoughts. And smile! Even a fake smile can release endorphins and help channel your energy to other things. You have to train yourself to recognize a negative inner monologue and to stop it in its tracks. Practice this daily, in bed in the morning, driving, or on your lunch break.

Limit Choices: We tend to lose our decision-making capabilities when we're not fully ourselves. My best friend will impose "No Decision Days" on me when I'm going through a tough time. It's true, I tend to be reckless, as we all can be when we're hurting. We want to stop the pain so desperately. I'm usually convinced sugar, shoes, and pretty little things will make me feel better. But it only makes me feel useless and regretful. Of course these are small decisions, but they still make an impact on our well-being. Big ones? No, no, let's leave those for a day when the sun is shining, our caffeine has kicked in, and we're ready to take the world by storm. No break-ups, big purchases, new jobs, moves, and for Pete's sake, no chopping off your hair or cutting in bangs. Just don't do it yet. There are a few decisions I will always allow you to make when you're down, though: Getting on a plane to Paris, buying a down comforter or down pillow if you don't already have one, and rapping off-beat in your pajamas in the kitchen into a wooden spoon. These are solid decisions.

Letting Others In

From seeking medication to asking a friend to stage a life-intervention, acknowledging we need help, asking for it, and accepting it can be some of the biggest steps we take on our way back to brave.

Acknowledging we need help is a huge step on the path towards healing. Trauma affects us, takes us down a peg or a few. We can be left holding pieces of our lives we never thought we'd see the edges of, with no instructions for gluing them back together or disposing of them safely. What a difficult thing to face in life.

Asking for help might be foreign to us. Most of us are good at helping others and terrible at receiving help. I'm not sure why this is, but it's unfortunate. If you are asking from a place of sincerity, people tend to respond from a place of sincerity. Most people want to help and will feel valued that you trusted them.

Accepting help is brave. Oh, so brave. Whatever kind of help it is, from a financial boost to help you through rough times or letting a friend come clean your house when you're working two jobs, it is a humbling and vulnerable thing to let someone so close to your life. This is okay. You can be humble, vulnerable, and strong at the same time. They are not mutually exclusive.

Of course I am no medical expert, but I will highly encourage you to find a nurturing doctor who listens and takes time and to seek their opinion. Medication, whether natural or pharmaceutical, can help you get back to a base level of functioning so you can have the energy and wherewithal to move forward. There is no shame in supplementing your care when needed.

We are adaptable people. That's a good and bad thing. When things are good, we are quick to accept a cushy lifestyle, easily adjusting. But we do the same thing when things are bad . . . we adapt and can become so used to the new situation that we forget. We forget that it hasn't always been this way. It doesn't always have to be this way. I just want you to remember that we are capable of growth and change. We are capable of moving forward, leaving behind, going on. Oh yes, we are. Oh yes, we will.

The Little Things

Happiness is everywhere, and free. Isn't that just the best? I love finding happiness along my path. See, happiness is different than joy. To me, joy is deep-down. A secret well of hope, desire, and an absolute knowing that life is good and worthwhile even when it's hard. That is joy. And cultivating joy is a life-long process. There comes a time when the "get through" needs to be put on the shelf and it's time to begin again.

Happiness, happiness is a spring in your step because the dew this morning felt warm instead of cold, and reminded you that spring is coming. A smile because you can see the steam coming off your tea and it's quite pretty. The way your dogs are beside themselves to see you when you get home. Little things that ease the day and make those tough times meaningful.

I believe that a happy life is defined by living life from that depth of joy instead of from the thin soil of fear. No roots grow there, my dears.

The skies are always blue behind the gray. That's a fact (I'm pretty sure; don't double-check, if it isn't, it's poetic license, okay?).

I believe in braids and baking and bravery and belonging and goodness-gracious, I believe in being nice and always saying yes to whipped cream. *Whole milk*, people. None of this skim-milk-living. I'm talking life, and living with verve and charm and gusto and grace and all the happy-pretty-messy you can muster.

I believe in leaning in and going big when things are getting tough and you're feeling small. I believe in taking deep breaths, getting up to watch sunrises, climbing mountains to feel the freedom in the forest. I believe in digging in and getting it done, and then having a cookie. *Cookies*, people. None of this always-dieting-living. I'm talking sugar-sweet, life-is-short living.

I believe in ballet and big sunglasses and buying coffee for strangers and braving snowstorms to play

board games around a fire. I believe in building each other up, bearing each other's burdens, and pie. Pie makes
everything better. And so does ice cream. Yes, and
sprinkles. Pie, with ice cream, and sprinkles. That's
the sort of life I'm talking—no one needs the whole
pie, just one piece, with extra happiness sprinkled
high.

I believe in being virtuous with equal amounts of vigor. I believe in
bucking the system, but only with good reason and good conscience. I believe in showing your scars when it will help others but never letting them be
the baggage you carry wherever you go. I'm talking a life of freedom with
your hands empty and heart splayed open and displayed for everyone to see
and admire.

And gosh darn it, I believe you are brave, and you are beautiful. If no one
else has told you, or you haven't heard it recently, or your heart has decided to
stop believing it, let me tell you: you are brave, and you are beautiful.

The best kinds of people are those who have gone through something
and not let it destroy them. I think it's one of the biggest hat tricks of life,
to pull a rabbit of hope out of a black hat of trauma. It creates a realness
that can't be faked, a depth of self that can be achieved in no other way. We
are carved deeper. And that is good, albeit painful. The getting of ourselves
"back" can be even more painful, but it is part of our life's work. It is here
we find the very art of living. It is easy to live well when things are within our
grasp.

I like mountains and I like valleys. I like being on top of the world and
I don't mind taking a breather on the side of the path on the way there. Life
is so demanding that I take the pressure off. No, I say, and shake my head.
That always helps. Just say it out loud and shake your head as many times as
you need.

Open doors. *Open doors.* That's both a directive and an open-hands philosophy for life. Opening doors invites open doors. Bravery begets bravery. Love attracts love. Do you see where I'm going with this? Give what you want to get. Go where you want to find it. Be there, be ready, be willing, and open doors.

Most of all, I love people who struggle and smile. I love people who struggle and remain soft. There is little braver in this world.

We live thinking our lives are small, our struggles insurmountable, our failures our name tags. Reject these lies. I refuse to believe that any human life is without worth, without place, and without a home for their heart.

Your life is so very valuable and your struggles are simply a means to an end. A refining, a polishing, a shining-up of your inner beauty. Oh what a precious thing, to be loved enough to be polished by the world. I think it's quite lovely.

Thing is, sometimes we get a little too comfortable stuck in the struggles. We stop fighting when we are wounded. No, my darling. That is not where we live life. That is where we get prepared for life, where we dig into the deeper parts of it, but not where we live our days out. We must fight until we rise, hang in there until we see the blessing.

Move through your life with strength and courage. Sometimes this feels physically demanding. It is difficult work and I make no excuse for that. But you are building character, fortitude, perseverance. The skills that allow you to keep going. Keep going. These will not all be wins. There will be days when you decide you are too sad to be strong, and I am okay with that. But I want you to know that you are the only one who can decide to be sad, or to be strong, and that you should use this power with care. It can destroy a life, you know.

And very often we choose things that aren't best for us. I've found that we always know what we need, deep down, but listening to it is the real work of it. Bringing who we are to the world, seeing what we find.

I have to keep surprising myself with bravery. Out-of-the-blue bravery.

• • • • • • • • • • • • • •

This world is my forest and I am the avid outdoorswoman

Trail-traipsing hiking boots, or running shoes or high heels

Denim coveralls stained with berry juice and honey

Or a dress embroidered with wildflowers

As I meander from a coffee-shop window seat

To a stone tower on the side of a mountain

I keep a tote bag on my shoulders

Empty, to fill with the time and space

That I collect in musty bookstores and Moroccan markets

Fragments of sunrise on Mount Fuji and sunset

At the Santa Monica Pier

I save these things because they are the dust

Of a thing called wanderlust that I never wish to lose

The whoosh of a bicyclist by me, the hum

Of a shopkeeper watering her flowers

And the persistent meows of a street cat are the soundtrack

To the screenplay I write in my head, my map

So I remember how to get back here,

Should I ever find the need to retrace my steps

To get somewhere new

I leave no signs, really, that I was here

Except perhaps if you listen closely when the wind trills

Even in the city, for I have found many a city to love

You may find me saying to you

"Come with me, darling, let's go seeking and find

Hidden amongst the most intricate tapestry of human life

The embroidered truth that our beautiful differences

Are what make the world worth discovering."

• • • • • • • • • • • • • •

The Actual Adventuring

I want an A-frame in the snowy mountains and a little vintage trailer for taking coast-to-coast the rest of the time. I like staying and going, leaving and coming and bringing and taking with me to remember. Oh, it is all so wonderful what you can find when you're adventuring with an open heart and a brave spirit.

What is adventuring? It's taking a drive. Taking a walk. Going somewhere new and seeing what you find. Getting up and going. This can be little or big. I love to take off on a Saturday and adventure to a new town, find a new thrift shop, a new bookstore. This is my summer routine. Adventuring is always a success because there is no agenda. If I find an old-fashioned photo booth, the adventure has been even more of a success, because they are one of my favorite things.

Vintage Photo Booths

Vintage photo booths are truly one of my favorite things in life. They are captivating and I cannot get enough of them. There was a photo strip on our fridge for ages growing up, my dad with his youthful smile and my brother with his eyes closed in all four frames. I will go well out of my way to find one, will shove every last dollar bill I have in to get as many photos as I can. These absolutely must be the vintage dip-and-dunk kind that gives you textured black and white paper with four small photos that come out wet and smelling of chemicals. These will last forever, unlike the new digitally printed ones on glossy photo paper that fade in days. Hopefully there's a little round stool and a curtain you can pull across the background or not for two different options. There is, of course, a black curtain you close off to the world to make the little booth dark. Be sure you're wearing cute shoes for the passers-by to see. Make a new face every flash and be silly. I like sunglasses on, kiss-blowing, side profiles, hands over face, surprised looks, and, of course, smooches if you happen to have your significant other with you. You'll have to wait about three minutes for the photo to process and pop into the little cubby. Be careful not to hit the "railing" inside as it can smudge your fabulous pictures. Hold carefully by the edges and blow on it a little until it is completely dry. Don't worry, the chemical scent goes away as soon as it dries.

I've accidentally trailed behind Morris dancers going from New England town green to town green to welcome spring. It was delightful and festive. I've taken the 101 and ended up at the Atlantic Ocean after a few hours' drive. I discovered a drink called the "White Hot Banana" that is a white chocolate-banana mocha served hot or iced. I've discovered the last haul of New England-made woven ribbons and you'd better bet I grabbed a stash. I've found live music to enjoy at lunch time, met the cutest couple who had the most glorious display of lilacs I've ever seen, found hidden historic treasures only whispered about by locals, and been gifted the most fabulously luscious armful of dahlias as big as my head by Joe, fisherman and gardener. He told me his secret, too, and I'll pass it along because how can I not? Crushed aspirin and fishmeal is what those dahlias live for.

While most of my adventuring is done within a day's drive, it is good for the spirit to wake up in a new place every once in a while. It is a little jump-start for the senses. If this is a friend's guest room a few streets over, go for it. If it's a trip to the Fjords, go for it (and bring Dramamine. Those cruises to see the Fjords aren't messing around). The theory is the same and works no matter where you lay your head. For adventuring a bit farther afield, it can be good to keep in mind that you may wish to spend the night and to keep an overnight bag handy. Or you may plan the adventure. Most years I travel to the nearest Garrison Keillor show and book a hotel or bed-and-breakfast. One bed-and-breakfast proprietor was so shocked I was alone she could hardly stand it and told me, "Well, the walls are soundproof if you do end up bringing someone back tonight." Um, no, I'm good. Just me, thanks. But I enjoy a good bed and a good breakfast just as much as any coupled-up traveler and for that I will not apologize. These quirks are the stuff of stories, the stuff of inspiration and awakening.

Adventuring Essentials

Go where the wind blows you. Get on a road and follow it until you find something new and interesting. That's how day trip adventuring works at its most basic level. Every part of the day is up for grabs. Go forth with an open heart, open eyes, open hands, and an open sunroof, if you have one. Don't forget the glamorous sunglasses, and I definitely approve of a silk scarf tied in your hair, too.

1) **Stop for Snacks and Drinks.** I love an ice cream from a random ice cream stand or an iced coffee from a little mom-and-pop shop. You can discover lots of culinary gems, and snacks and drinks are easier on the budget than whole meals. Take the time to sit on the front step and take in the surroundings.

2) **Bring Two Tote Bags.** Bring an empty one to carry in your purse until you need it. You'll want to slip your sunglasses in it, literature you pick up from that cool artist's open studio you found or a business card from the funky little bakery. In the other tote bag, keep supplies for the day in your car. I suggest sunscreen, bug spray, a change of comfy shoes or flip flops, a hat, bottled water, a "just in case" snack, a book to read, and a notebook and pencil.

3) **Choose Your Tunes—or Skip 'em.** Some days I love to adventure with all of the windows down and the radio blasting. Other days, I find the quiet soothing to my soul. There is something about the open road that seems to inspire inner thought, don't you think? But I'm not going to lie, Bruce Springsteen or the Beach Boys make pretty good adventuring companions.

4) **Take Photos—or Skip 'em.** Sometimes I want to capture every detail of my day. Other days, I want my heart to capture all of the memories, so I leave my camera behind. Sometimes I dig out my notebook and pencil to sketch instead. Do whatever feels right at the time.

5) **Stop at Quirky Places, Tourist Stops, and All of Those Things You Said You'd Do One Day.** Stop at that cute diner. The florist with the beautiful flowers out front every day. Pop into the record store, even if you don't have a record player. Stop at places like the Postage

Stamp Museum or the Toaster Museum or that roadside stand that claims to have the World's Largest Hamburger. Because you're adventuring, right? So be *adventurous*.

6) **Be Incredibly Kind to Everyone You Meet and Enjoy the Spirit of the Day.** Enough said!

Solo Adventuring

Most of my adventuring is done alone, because it can be tough to find a good adventuring partner. Being alone allows you to see everything through your own eyes, your own circumstances. It gives you your own stories. Of course you'll want to stay safe while adventuring alone but strangers are very helpful most of the time, especially if you keep your spirit open to it. Obviously, I'm not suggesting you hitchhike, but I am suggesting you ask strangers to take your picture. This is such a great way to start a conversation, too. Despite having many pictures of stranger's thumbs with me blurry in the background, I've started many good conversations this way. Found many good poetry prompts. I love stories, I love swapping them and hearing what people divulge to a stranger. It's funny, isn't it, how sometimes we are more honest with a passer-by than with ourselves. So I tuck them away, and keep their honesty safe. And I share my own. It's the give-and-take of life that fills us to the brim when we are out there living. It's what brave gives us.

Yes, it takes some guts to go solo adventuring. It takes clearing your schedule for a few hours on Saturday morning or Sunday afternoon to go outside of your comfort zone. We feel awkward alone sometimes. I'm not quite sure where we've developed this narrative. Our self is the only constant companion we have, and we should treat ourselves with respect.

Start by soaking up small moments alone. Get coffee by yourself and actually sit down. Get it in a china mug and sit there until you finish it. Open your eyes and ears. Take it all in. Sip as if you are a movie star, that's what

I tell myself. I focus on the beauty of the coffee, the feel of my hand in the handle. I adjust the curve of my fingers to be graceful, purse my lips to be attractive. I sink into the moment, become fully aware of the details of it. I pretend I am a painting, a sculpture, a poem. That perhaps someone in a quiet corner is painting me, sculpting me, writing me. If it makes you nervous to not have your hands busy, bring a book or magazine. Bring a journal and write. But not your phone, darling. Being on your phone while you're alone makes it look like you are uncomfortable, and that is not the case, right?

Then, work up to a movie by yourself. It's quite delightful once you let yourself be there alone. Load up on the snacks you like, no sharing required. Laugh when you want to, instead of when your partner is. Stay for the credits if you want. I am a seasoned movie-alone-goer. I even go to the drive-in movies, a classic date or family-night place, by myself, without hesitation (though on Saturday nights I have to pay for two tickets to get a car spot, which feels a bit unfair!). I stare at the sky as long as I want and come back to the movie when I'm ready. Watching a movie outdoors is magical, and I'm not willing to give that up because everyone else is busy.

Finally, go on an afternoon trip. I suggest starting out going somewhere within a 45-minute radius of your hometown. Go anywhere 45 minutes away. Half an hour is within our normal routine, but those extra 15 minutes should take you to adventuring territory. Your mission is to have coffee somewhere you have never been. You're adventuring alone. You're doing it, you brave and beautiful one, you. Isn't it exhilarating? Can't you feel the wind coming back under your wings?

Group Adventuring

Of course, group adventuring is exciting for all of the opposite reasons of solo adventuring. Being in a group allows you to see many different perspectives and to share a common story. When I went to Ecuador on a mission trip, my best friend and I met up with fifty other twenty-somethings from all around the world that we'd never met before. Let's just say some of those bus rides were adventurous. But I ended up hiking underneath a waterfall in the rain forest and getting thoroughly soaked on my twentieth birthday. Believe it or not there was another girl in my group who had the same birthday as me, and some friends tried to buy us a birthday cake at the largest market in South America. Somehow "Natalie and Mariah" became "Miriam" on the cake. Our Spanish friends serenaded us and we celebrated for three . . . Natalie, Mariah, and Miriam. You can't make those memories up.

We had a free afternoon, and for some reason I decided it was a great idea to lead a group of three twenty-something fresh-faced girls who spoke zero Spanish on an excursion. In Quito, Ecuador. We hailed a taxi. We managed to tell him we wanted to go shopping. We shopped, we ate, we used the internet café to tell our parents of our adventure so they could be horrified at our lack of self-awareness, and managed to make it back to campus safely. And, might I add, with a few fashionable new additions to our wardrobes. Oh, did I mention that we needed them? Our luggage got lost and my friend and I had to make do with the clothes we were wearing when we left America four days prior. We walked to the "Super-Maxi" (the grocery-store, I know, I know) and managed to find washcloths and underwear. I still have nightmares about that underwear. (Sometimes culture shock manifests at unexpected moments—like when you realize the local underwear is cut for a butt that in no way resembles your own.)

Then there's the hat. The hat my friend Gregg should have bought. We still mention it to this day. Although we only met on that trip and have seen each other a handful of times in the years since, we still randomly text, "THE HAT!" with true remorse. It just looked so good on him. There's the warm sweet milk we thought was coffee for days. Until we noticed a small bowl with a lid on it and powdered coffee in the middle of the table that we were meant to add to our warm milk. There were the hotdogs in eggs for breakfast. And tree-tomato juice and guinea pigs for dinner.

Group adventuring comes with caveats, of course. You're stuck on the bus. You're stuck in a room with the snorer. The group leader has a voice you simply can't stand. But don't you see? That's the adventure. You're in it.

Mother-Daughter Adventuring

Mother-daughter adventuring is one of my favorites, and a habit my mother and I have cultivated since I was very young. It started with Saturday morning garage sale and donut days, and eventually ended in across-the-Pond adventures. The memory bank we've filled is priceless.

I was obsessed with bed-and-breakfasts at a young age and read every guidebook about Michigan bed-and-breakfasts our library had. Mom and I planned out a road trip from our Indiana home to a Michigan bed-and-breakfast. Then we went farther afield, to Chicago for an exhibit of Jackie Kennedy's dresses from The White House years. Finally, when I was in high school, we flew to Paris.

Paris, where I paid for the bathroom at the Sacre Coeur three times because I was intimidated by the literal hole in the ground with two foot marks on either side. Paris, where we ran after our tour van with baguettes in hand to flag them down because we were late. In our small Parisian hotel room, closing the bathroom door wasn't an option when you were actually sitting on the toilet because . . . knees. People have knees. People in Paris have knees, too, right, or am I missing something?

Mother-daughter adventuring is unique. People love a mother-daughter duo. We champion them, love to see them getting along and, gasp, traveling. Seeing the world together. Making memories that only the two of you share. Life is short and connection is constantly being interrupted. These stories of traveling together keep us connected across distance, across time, across growing up and growing old, and they hold us together.

Plan a trip. Book a bus ticket, hop on a train. Meet in Chicago at Christmastime. Do Broadway in the Spring. Go see the orchid exhibit at the botanical garden, the film festival a few towns over. Go to a bed-and-breakfast, or share a hotel room with a bathroom door that won't close, because that is the stuff memories are made of. That is the stuff of adventuring.

Living in Love: Relationships

"PERFECT LOVE DRIVES OUT FEAR." 1 JOHN 4:18

It's a tricky thing, this business of two hearts walking together. I admit that many days my own heart needs tending enough for two of us. Still, relationships allow us to "divide the burdens and multiply the joys." Isolation is a slow death. We are created to live in relationship. Trust me when I say that friendship and chosen-family can fill a heart to overflowing even if there is no romantic love in our lives. But romantic love is quite nice indeed, I think, and nothing to be ashamed of desiring. All types of love require sacrifice and vulnerability. And bravery.

On Being Brave and Baggage

Allowing oneself to be loved is brave. It truly, truly is. Being loved takes a lot of those deep-heart things Mr. Rodgers and our parents tried to teach us but that along the way we unlearn and undo. Being loved requires humility. It requires strength. It requires a sense of self, as well as a sense of surrender. Being loved is a selfless act, really, because you are giving your heart to another. That means they can be reckless with it, unkind, and potentially downright damaging. Oh, to give that power to another is a deep, deep thing.

It is worth it, though; I believe that with everything in me. A life without love drains your being. All of these things it takes to be loved are the real stuff of life. It's what makes life worth living, what feeds the age-old parts of our souls that exist solely to love and be loved. It is a trust exercise. Others might not be strong enough to catch you, but that doesn't mean you aren't strong. It is the letting-in we are working on, the being strong in our selves.

Loving, too, is brave. It means putting aside your own selfishness. More than that, it means putting another's best interest above yours. Constantly. No wonder it is a scary thing to commit to for life. It is much easier to wait until the infatuation passes and then move on to the next "high" we get from the next new crush. But that is a walls-up defense mechanism, and a heart constantly on the defense is not lovely or particularly loveable. We drag along this baggage and hope no one notices, but it becomes quite obvious when we're tripping over it ourselves.

What is "baggage" really? We all know what it means instinctively, but trying to define it and unpack it, so to speak, can be a much more difficult task. I think baggage really comes down to *heart-damage and fear.* Of course heart-damage and fear come in many, many different 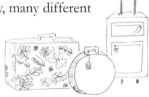 shapes and sizes, but the bottom line of baggage is what it has done to your spirit and how you carry that forward. Some people can have a whole closet full of luggage but it's not baggage because they don't carry it in their hearts. Others might only have one grudge or bad experience, but it goes everywhere with them.

It takes hard heart-work to unpack baggage. It takes real effort, physical pain often, perhaps financial investment, and most of all, it takes willingness. Awareness and willingness. These are tough words, and even tougher to live, I know. But it's the only way we can learn to love ourselves (again, perhaps). To truly find happiness with another we must love ourselves. You know how on airplanes they tell you to put your own oxygen mask on first before assisting others? You're no good to others if you aren't whole-hearted yourself.

Fear has no place in relationships. Fear can be external or internal, and based on reality or all in our imaginations. External fear is obviously the fear of physical things, such as harm or heights. Internal fear is a deeper foe, a hard one to root out. Often, we've lived with internal fear for so long that it seems a part of us; oh, internal fear can easily undermine a relationship. It can be hard to name. Hard to tame.

You will never be successful in love or life when you respond out of fear. I hate to say it, but I can because I know it to be true. Life is hard. You've developed your coping mechanisms, I understand. I have mine, too. Fear is a coping mechanism. "Coping mechanism" is not always a bad term; we need them to keep going through tough things. The trouble is when the coping mechanisms we choose are damaging to ourselves or others.

Much fear comes from not being well-loved in the past. We become afraid of commitment, of showing our true selves in case it isn't wanted, of saying "I love you," of seeking the sort of person we actually want or being the person we actually are because in the past we were told, "No." We were shown that commitment doesn't exist, that we aren't good enough or that we will always repeat our mistakes. These lies are ugly.

Why would we take advice on love from someone who doesn't know the meaning? Why put words of condemnation on our hearts because someone else didn't feel secure? I will choose new words. I will choose whole and healthy, happy and loved. Look in the mirror. Speak beauty over yourself. Let me start you off: I see purpose when I look at you. I see designed for greatness and I see made to love well.

● ● ● ● ● ● ● ● ● ● ● ● ● ●

I gaze amongst the fields of broken pieces
And gather basketsful to bring back to you,
To empty on the table and to say,

"Let's create something beautiful, and new,"
When we are finished admiring the beauty that can
Only come from broken pieces, we'll go down to the water

Let's get in the canoe, darling, for even though
This art is new, it is made of old things, for which we have no need
Now that we are whole again inside
So let's take this down to the beaver pond
And set it afloat
They might have some use for it, there

Let me build into your life, dear friend
Where you see only empty land
I will help you lay the foundations for the most remarkable
Home that was ever built for stargazing
And Sunday dreaming
Enjoy the view from here and store it away deep within you
For storms and travels and for days when your head
Seems disconnected from your heart: remember this view

Let your facial expressions tell a love story
Not a mystery, for the world is too full of dark alleys
And brick walls and I say, be like a little white picket fence
With a gate and walk through the town giving away samples

Of what it means to be generous, and loved, and true

Stand on tiptoe and stare into the horizon of this
Great big beautiful world and know that should you ever
Feel lonely and I am not near, go out onto the
Noisy, pulsing streets, find someone with starry eyes
Take their hand and say, "Let's row across the pond."

• • • • • • • • • • • • •

Hard Hearts and Hard-Knock Lives

We harden our hearts at the drop of a word or at the hint of a facial expression. It seems we are always looking for ways to harden our hearts. Our vices are generally just ways to harden our hearts against unwanted feelings. We harden our hearts by shutting people down or out, by not giving them a chance, by living with our own comfortable assumptions about people, by pretending we don't care or don't love or don't notice.

Anything can break our hearts, really. Yours may have broken long ago in your childhood or it may have been your latest breakup. It may happen daily or it may have happened once and that was it for you. Lovers, friends, family, careers, injuries . . . all sorts of things can cause us to harden our hearts right up. A hard heart is a broken one, but we don't like to acknowledge that. A hard heart may hide behind a façade of strength, but our hearts are no fools.

Sometimes we choose to harden our hearts, which may hurt even more because we know deep down that we're doing it to ourselves. Choosing to stay when we should leave, choosing to leave when we should stay, choosing words that aren't the ones we really want to say, choosing to close our eyes tight and hum loudly and try to cover the silence of a breaking heart.

Let me tell you something: A hard-knock life is no excuse for a hard heart. In fact, it's the opposite. What an opportunity to show the world your beauty and bravery! Bravery doesn't come from doing easy things. Bravery is hard-won and beauty is the reward of a whole heart. Don't let your brokenness define you. Don't let it become you. A hard heart doesn't heal properly. A hard heart scabs over and scar tissue takes over, and it's really quite an ugly scene. No one tells you that part, but you can feel it. It hurts, and can be bumped open with the slightest touch. It's a wound you carry everywhere. Shrapnel of the heart.

We love to build walls and castles and towers and moats. We love to lock up our dragons, but we forget that when we lock them up inside our walls we are still living with them. They are breathing fire in our direction. The soot is on the inside of our own throats. Oh, this is no fairy tale. This is a fight for our lives.

I suggest we change the story. What if instead of building walls, castles, towers, and moats, we built bridges, ladders, and boats? Let the dragons go, my dears. Let love win.

You can see a broken heart, did you know that? It emanates. It shows in your countenance. It walks into the room before you, it takes over your laugh, it takes over your eyes. It affects you physically.

What if we practiced softening our hearts in the face of fear? How? How do we heal a broken heart? I won't tell you it's easy or quick. I won't tell you it's painless or proven. But here's what I do know: It is worthwhile to heal properly. It is essential.

Minor Breaks

Some things, like hearts, don't look broken when you look at them from a certain angle. But tilt the light just a little bit to see the fault line. These are minor breaks. Losing a job, a lover, a friend. Healing a minor broken heart is a slow process until all of a sudden it happens in a flash. You might even miss the moment it heals. But first you must grieve.

Remember, no hardening of your heart. Actual examples of metaphorically hardening your heart include: Going out to date someone, anyone, else immediately; chopping off all of your hair; exhausting yourself at work; going into debt with online shopping sprees; and the list goes on. No, none of that. Grieving requires going to the pain, not escaping. Pain isn't pretty, and we like pretty.

But go there. Sit with it for a bit. Name it. Write it down. Cry it out. Dance it off. If you literally want to lie on your bed and throw a toddler-tantrum, do it. Get your bucket list out and cross a few things off. We're looking for actions without bad consequences, and ideally things that are actually constructive. These things are the brave ones. Anyone can put up walls, but you, you were made for more. You will see the sun shining again. And it will be the most glorious thing you've ever seen. You'll feel alive again, you'll feel your heart beating whole again, and you'll be there. You'll be there.

Major Breaks

Major breaks are deeply broken hearts. They may have healed improperly the first time around or are such profound wounds they need trauma care. This is okay. You are still okay. Hang tough with me here, because I've been there. Deeply broken hearts can take years to heal, but the sooner you start the sooner you'll be healthy. Counseling is my number one recommendation for major heartbreaks. Friends can do this to an extent, but friends can only take so much hashing-out of a situation before they get hashed-out. A mentor or counselor is your best bet. Some heartbreaks will require constant care, more than once a week, because a heart can fall apart a lot in a week when it is weak. If you can't find a mentor or afford a counselor, I highly recommend you write out the story. Write out every detail. Every emotion. Every memory. Getting it out of your head is such a relief. Then you'll have a tangible representation of your heartbreak, which is important for closure. What you choose to do with this story is up to you. Shred it, burn it, ship it out to the ocean on the waves, share it with friends; whatever feels right.

One of my most useful tools for a heart check-in is visualization. Close your eyes and picture your heart. What do you see? It can be good to draw this as well. Check in with your heart often and you'll see progress. Eventually, you won't need to close your eyes to picture your heart. You'll feel it full within you, beating well and strong.

Letting go, even of hard things and heartbreak, is scary. It is change, and we are generally averse to change. Don't be afraid. Keep moving forward into the future. A soft heart is one that the world finds attractive. You are moving into better, and best. I promise.

When you've healed your own heart, it's this strange phenomenon that you'll walk around seeing hard hearts everywhere you go. You'll want to build bridges. You'll want to reach out your hands and take theirs. You'll want to drown their dragons in the moat. This shows progress, yes. But it is a test. See, we can't do that for others. We can try, oh my, can we try. We can spend all of our energy on something they may not want. Many of us, we're friends with our dragons. We pet them and feed them and keep them close. And trying to tackle someone else's dragon may very well release yours again. Lead them to resources, gently, share your own story, but don't fight their dragons. Dragons don't go down easy.

This segues into one more little note: Stay away from fixer-upper relationships. No, no, none of that. We are seeking another soft heart, another moving-forward heart. We are seeking whole-hearted love. The good news is that whole-hearted love can be cultivated, starting wherever you are.

On Wanting and Being Wanted

I wish I didn't have to write this section, you guys. I wish we were all wanted, loved, chosen, cherished, and cheered for every day of our lives. But there come times in all of our lives when we don't feel wanted, or when there is someone we aren't super-keen on being wanted by, or we don't want the one we're with. Oh, oh, oh it hurts so badly.

Sometimes it is obvious we aren't wanted. We're told straight-up, or we're cheated on, or we're left at the altar, or we're given a brown envelope with "papers." We know. Other times, we aren't told with words or big dynamite-y-actions. We're told with fewer whispers, higher walls, and gradual goodbyes. Until goodbye is all we're left with. I was never good at goodbyes.

Sometimes, though, it's the other way around, and we're not really-sure-sure in our heart of hearts that we want someone. It's a terrible thing to be loved more than you love someone else. And it's a terrible thing to love someone more than they love you. The internal conflict leads to desperation. Desperation never made for a strong relationship or a healthy heart.

I know it seems strange to say there could be "too much" love, but you know what I mean, right? This may be smother-love, coddling, and allowing you to be soft all the time. Or it may simply be someone who is at a different point in their life than you are and is ready to go all-in when you aren't. It is equally taxing for a heart to invest more than it receives, and in the end it is damaging to both parties. It is one of those times we have to be truly-true with ourselves and assess the situation in daylight. Love yourself enough, darling. Love yourself enough to not need to be wanted. To wait for someone who wants to want you.

Have you ever not-wanted to be wanted by someone? It's odd, really. Quite an unsettling feeling. I've had boyfriends who followed me around like puppies insistent on chewing my shoelaces. That was an easy no. But when you're hugging someone and your heart is nagging you, it's uncomfortable. Of course it's tempting to shake it off because hugs are amazing, duh. We like being able to get hugs at any time of day just for the asking or taking or giving. But that isn't enough.

Breaking someone's heart is a terrifying experience. It rips you apart a bit, if you really realize it. No one has much sympathy for the instigator of a broken heart, but truth is there's really never just one broken heart. It's like a hug—you give one, you get one. Broken hearts, too. I'm not saying you should console the breaker-of-your-heart. I am saying that most of us face a time or two in life when we must be the bearers of news that will break a heart. So I am also saying, don't break hearts selfishly. Don't do it flippantly or graceless-ly. Do it with all of the spirit you can muster at the moment, all of the grace your momma gave you. These are hearts we're talking about, and they are worth handling with care, always.

How do we know when to dig in and dig deeper, and when to let go and let fly?

Digging in deeper is almost-always the go-to plan. Love requires an oc-casional grand gesture, running-after-you-at-the-airport kinda stuff. But what we really need is the dying-to-self grand gesture. The actually meaningful one, like telling your boss you can't work on Sundays because sitting in a pew with your family is more important. The Internet timer because real life is more important than screen-time reading about strangers' lives. It requires digging deeper into your own heart. Coming clean with yourself about your feelings and what you want. Again, this isn't easy.

See, some of us need to work on staying and some of us need to work on leaving. I tend to be a stay-er. I love possibility. I love potential. I love falling in love with fantasy. And boys love to live up to possibility for a girl for as long as they can manage. Until it all falls apart. One or the other is left having to break our hearts.

to do:
stay
OR
leave

To let ourselves leave, or to let someone else go, is one of the nitty-gritty parts of life. It's another strange phenomenon that after letting go usually comes regret. I wish letting go came instantly with freedom, but the fear comes first, followed by regret, and finally, freedom.

Outside my window, there's a little tin roof over a door, and above that roof is the larger roof, home to a nest of little birds. Let me tell you, when those birds start learning how to fly, they are literally scared-shitless. The little roof is covered in poop from the frightened little birdies being pushed out of the nest. That part is scary. Eventually they fly, but before that, they're shaking in their little birdie-boots. You'll feel that. And then you'll fly.

The bottom line is truthfulness. With ourselves. With others. Keeping our heart whole and keeping track of it. It is hard to bring our hearts with us. I'm prone to leaving mine on the top shelf of my closet with my fanciest shoes and my smallest handbags. Sometimes I have to put a note on the door, "Bring your heart." Today may be the day you need it more than ever.

BRING YOUR heart

"ALL THAT YOU ARE MAKES ME HAPPY. I LOVE YOU." —LOUIS TO ROSE IN FRENCH FILM *LA POPULAIRE*

(The clothes! All of the velvet hairbows! The PINK TYPEWRITER! It's like *Legally Blonde* set in the 1950s and in France, which I could not adore more.)

Whole-Hearted Loving

Whole-hearted loving is such a beautiful thing. Life is short and there is no time for half-hearted loving. I have no heart for that (ha). In fact, half-hearted loving isn't really loving at all. When two people have faced all of their past hurts and fears and said, "Here I am," it is so intensely intimate. It is so different from what the world gives us. We are seen, accepted, chosen, and cherished. This is love. This is what we are seeking.

I am no expert at this, obviously. I am not sure there is expert status when it comes to this. But I haven't done all of this broken-hearted research for nothing. I love love and I love loving. Even after seeing love leave me so many times. I do not blame myself for that, nor do I blame the love I gave and received. For that I blame broken hearts, bad timing, and bad weather. You can blame bad weather for just about anything. But no matter; love is still worthy of effort in my opinion. A whole-hearted person is one who sees your effort, who sees what you are bringing to the table and raises you one, out of love. "Let us outdo one another in showing love," the Bible says *(Romans 12:10)*. Yes, this is what I mean. Whole means whole. It means, I'll bring all of me, you bring all of you, and we'll do all of this together. We'll do good, bad, and ugly, together.

Finding this from the beginning is the best, of course, but it doesn't always happen that way. Either way, it requires nurturing. Cultivating whole-hearted loving will be specific to your relationship, but it boils down to this: Doing everything with kindness and love. Everything. Kindness. Love. That means taking out the trash, unclogging the garbage disposal, doing the *stuff* of life with kindness and love. It is funny to me that we will go above and beyond if we have the accountability of someone unrelated to us, say a roommate or houseguest. We treat them with the utmost respect and trip over ourselves to give them a great experience. Yet for the ones we hold dearest, we can let even the smallest kindnesses slide.

hang it up

I once dated a guy who had a very demanding job with very long hours as a pharmacist. But there was a stop sign on his way home that became the "hang it up" stop sign. It's hard to shake work off immediately, but by the time you're halfway home and pass the stop sign, you mentally "hang up" and stop all of the work stresses of the day. Then you shake out the kinks the rest of the way home. We didn't invent this technique, but it works if you practice it daily.

I like to have a cup of caffeinated tea at about 3 p.m. to get me over the workday hump so I don't arrive home grumpy and with zero energy for home chores and projects. Married friends of mine make a cup of coffee after the kids go to bed so they can have energy to spend time together. The extra caffeine boost can really make relationships better.

Like anything else, whole-hearted loving takes work and practice. It takes awareness. It takes discipline, and a little extra caffeine. It takes investing in your own heart and taking care of its health. If you have nothing left at the end of a day to devote to love, something is more wrong with your priorities than with your relationship, I'd venture to say. Ouch, I know that hurts. We all get out of whack sometimes, so just take a deep breath and commit yourself to getting back in whack. That sounds weird, but it's what it takes. A decision-point. A "Jesus-take-the-wheel" moment. Those are such good moments. I am cheering you on.

So bring your heart with you on this journey we call life. Bring it with you, taped and stapled and scarred, but whole.

Capturing Memories

Journaling

I'm a writer, so journaling comes naturally to me. But even if it doesn't come naturally to you, I think you will find your life benefits from it. There is something about putting your life down on paper that helps you let it go or hold it closer. There is a freedom in getting it out of your head. Our heads are precarious places to keep much of anything for a long period of time. Journaling offers a 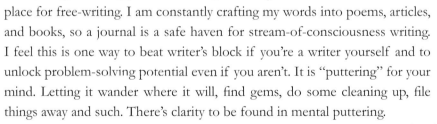 place for free-writing. I am constantly crafting my words into poems, articles, and books, so a journal is a safe haven for stream-of-consciousness writing. I feel this is one way to beat writer's block if you're a writer yourself and to unlock problem-solving potential even if you aren't. It is "puttering" for your mind. Letting it wander where it will, find gems, do some cleaning up, file things away and such. There's clarity to be found in mental puttering.

Choosing a journal is intensely personal. Find one that speaks to you. Inside, write the date you started the journal (leave room for an ending date as well, so you can easily organize your journals by date, should you desire), your age if you dare, and a prayer, quote, or words of wisdom for the journal.

I usually find a standard journal isn't quite enough for a whole year, so I look for thicker ones. A ribbon is essential to me, and I like ones with hard backs so they balance on my lap in bed and can take a travel beating. I remember my first journal; an opalescent white 3x5 size notebook where I wrote endlessly about my first crush. My brother found it and started shouting it around the house in a mushy voice and I was mortified. I remember the horror in my bones to this day. But it didn't turn me off from journaling. Nor did the time a boyfriend found a list of reasons I didn't like him (bad Natalie) but that was quite obviously a break-up that was fast coming.

One friend burns her journals when she's done with them, because she can't stand to look back on her inner thoughts. I keep mine, and love to read back through them to see the goodness of God shining through, to see how pieces of life fit together in good time, to remind myself that I have grown and that perspective is a valuable gift of age. Many times my journal preaches back to me, as if I wrote it for myself before I knew I would need to re-read it. I see that life is cyclical, that seasons come and go, that happiness always returns, and that joy can always be found.

Try journaling. See what you find. See where your soul takes you. See where words on paper can go that words said out loud can't.

Celebrating the Seasons

I live in Vermont, where winters are glorious. From inside, at least, cozied up near a woodstove, with layers and layers of wool and blankets and a steady supply of fresh hot cocoa and chocolate chip cookies delivered to you. Or from the ski slopes, if you can afford the lift ticket prices (and the potential broken bones). Otherwise, winter in Vermont can be a rough-around-the-edges,

desperate-in-the-spirit time for many of us. It is very easy to become a hermit in winter. Luckily, many special occasions take place in winter to lift our spirits and assuage our reclusive tendencies.

The holiday season starts with Thanksgiving, which may or may not bring snow, but is usually cold enough for a nice fire in the fireplace. That comforting crackling warmth seems to echo the happy hearts brought together in thankful repose. I often look around the table at Thanksgiving and hold the year's changes in my heart. Who is around the table now, added, and who is missing? Whose faces are etched a little deeper and whose have found new buoyancy? I love Thanksgiving and will always dress up the table as much as I can in colors of deep scarlet, burnt sienna, and of course, gold. There is no silver at a Thanksgiving table in my mind; it is a holiday for gold. Place cards are a fixture of my Thanksgiving table. I usually include a quotation on the back about thankfulness, or ask everyone to write what they are most thankful for on the back of their card. Don't let anyone go home after dinner; it's time for espresso or port and games. Good, wholesome board games, I'm talking about. Bring out the dominoes, the Scrabble, or charades. Make more memories. I might suggest karaoke, but after my own Great Thanksgiving Karaoke Debacle of 2011, I'm reluctant to add it to my list of approved activities for the holiday, and that's all I'll say about that.

• • • • • • • • • • • • • •

I do not know why pears choose to ripen this time of year
But I am grateful.
I do not know how far the church bells carry or if they like their song
But I am grateful.
I do not know where the stars lay their heads when they get tired
But I am grateful.

I am grateful for hands in mine and for feathers in nests

And even still I am grateful for letting go and flying.

I am grateful for the dawn of spring and cloudless skies

And even still I am grateful for snowshoes and silver linings.

I do not know the weight of time or the texture of happiness

But even still I am grateful because

This year I have learned that loving is brave

And being loved is even braver.

See this I know for certain:

That being brave is one of the most beautiful things

A heart could spend a lifetime doing

Here in this someday nervous world

Hoping for a heaven.

• • • • • • • • • • • • •

Then we're into a miraculous season: the advent of Christmas. There is nothing more romantic than the Christmas season in New England, to be sure. I've had a Florida Christmas before, and while it is lovely in its own way (a boat parade with the boats decked out and lit up, anyone?), it isn't the same as a good old-fashioned winter Christmas. Here in New England there are still drive-through nativities with actors and live camels. There are little yellow candles in the window of every 1800s house (and that's a lot of windows). Still carolers who come a'wassailing. Still a tree-lighting ceremony on Main Street and every shop window still decked out in real greenery and white lights. How romantic a scene to wander through, hand in hand with a lover, or warm in your heart by yourself, seeking treasures for those you love and feeling full to the brim of the beauty of life.

I always have an advent wreath at home, and I usually make it myself. This year I asked my friends, who are florists, if they made and sold them. She said they used to, but advent wreaths have fallen out of favor. I'm not sure how this is possible, but the tradition lives on in my house. The small gold wreath is decorated with greens and ribbons. It holds 4 or 5 candles, one for each of the 4 Sundays of Advent, and most have an additional "Christ" candle in the mid-  dle that you light on Christmas Eve. Advent readings and books can be found to enhance your experience of the tradition. You can light the candles every night, or only every Sunday. Either way, the shining wreath and the glow of family faces gathered 'round is good for the soul and the spirit of Christmas.

For Christmas Eve church service I try to find one vintage piece to make my outfit really pop. A vintage fur hat, a vintage black silk dress, a vintage ca- plet, a vintage floor-length plaid Pendleton wool skirt, a vintage brooch . . . these are a few of the things I've worn over the years. In my family we do Christmas on Christmas Eve night after church. A big dinner commences, with Swedish meatballs and all the traditional Swedish trimmings. Then we retire to the living room, read the Christmas story in the Bible, and sing a few songs while my dad plays his guitar. Finally, it's time to open presents. It is usually around midnight by this time, so technically Christmas Day, I suppose. There are trays of snacks all around and our traditional dessert drink of orange sherbet floating in cranberry juice. It tastes like Christmas. Everyone eventually settles down and goes to bed, but there is still excitement to be had in the morning. Stockings are found filled and we enjoy a lazy breakfast and spend the day in pajamas.

Of course, those are only the major winter holidays, but the stretch of New Year's Day to Valentine's Day can be the longest part of winter, so we make up our own fun. Have an ice fishing party, as friends of mine do. Round up as many plaid blankets and vintage plaid thermoses as you can. Bake a hundred hearty oatmeal raisin cookies. Find a beautiful little winter scene, fill the back of the pickup with pillows and blankets, and let everyone pile in to the back to watch the tip-ups go off when fish bite. For my birthday, you are all invited to go ice skating after church. I will bring pink cupcakes in leopard print wrappers and we'll buy hot chocolate with extra marshmallows. Why yes, I do have pom-poms on my ice skates like my mom's did in the seventies when she was an

Ice-capade at her high school. That's a hockey cheerleader, on the ice. How I would have loved to have seen her in those glory days! Instead, I wear her letter jacket, put pom-poms on my ice skates, and wear little skirts with tights and legwarmers to skate, because isn't that just adorable?

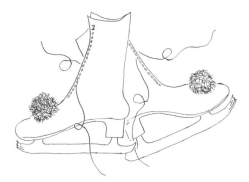

And suddenly it's Valentine's Day and the sun sets higher even though the days are still cold, and the heart warms a little at the thought of spring. And we get to celebrate romance and love. I love a holiday to celebrate love, and will never indulge those grouches who find it a manufactured holiday. There are two ways to do Valentine's Day: Going all out with the romance or keeping it casual with pajamas, takeout food, a bottle of champagne, a movie, and a (few) box(es) of chocolates. I have no problems with either of these options and therefore love this holiday. Even when I'm single. In fact, maybe even especially when I'm single, I adore this day.

I bake pink cupcakes, string hearts everywhere, make glittery valentines for all of my friends and their kids, buy as much pink candy as I can, order fresh flowers to make my heart sing, and pop pink champagne because any excuse for pink champagne is a good one. If I have a significant other for the holiday, I don't expect anything, but instead, choose to give. Men get overwhelmed at the "musts" of the holiday, but I hold none of them. Instead, I think of ways to shower love on him and to celebrate the love that he brings into my life. Any extra romantic gestures for me are icing on the cake. I skip through this day with a heart that holds love high in its many forms.

But Easter, Easter is my favorite holiday. Yes, I love it even more than Christmas. Easter is spring, it's my colors, it's a hat-wearing holiday and a new-dress holiday, and oh it makes my spirit soar. I hand-make Easter cards and exchange Easter baskets with my dear friend. I have vintage, tiny pastel table-setting Easter baskets that I fill with grass and goodies to set the table. Of course, there have to be mini daffodils and pussywillows in the centerpiece, because what is more cute and enticing for spring? Everything is light yellow, candy pink, mint green, and robin's egg blue. I always buy a new fascinator to wear to Easter Sunday church. Men and women alike are always complimenting my hats and fascinators, and the women usually say they wish they could pull them off. They can . . . if they try. Most are too intimidated to try. The good news is there are essentially no rules for ladies wearing hats. There may be a few guidelines, but generally women are allowed to wear hats indoors and outdoors and to all occasions, so don't fret!

How to Be Fascinating

A hat or fascinator is delightful and intriguing, don't you think? It's unique, vintage, ever-so Princess-y, and entirely fun for the wearer and those who may admire the lovely creation. A fascinator is a darling fashion accessory for any fancy occasion. Popularized by one of my fashion favorites, Duchess Catherine, these small headpieces can be simple or elaborate, but must always be elegant with a touch of whimsy. Fascinators are generally attached to hair combs, headbands, or thin elastics (these are worn at the nape of the neck, not under your chin). They are miniature works of art, usually handmade with care using horsehair, netting, silk, flowers, beads, jewels, and feathers. Wear a fascinator to special occasions, such as weddings, parties, derby races, bridal or baby showers, and the like. Duchess Catherine, or as I prefer to call her, Princess Kate, wears fascinators frequently when meeting with dignitaries and guests. They can be worn in all seasons, so long as they coordinate with your outfit and the weather. Fascinators are usually worn on the right side of the head, just above the eyebrow, on the side where there is less hair from the part. You can wear a fascinator with your hair down or up, and this helps you choose an appropriately sized fascinator. Hair down or half-down can carry a larger fascinator, whereas a ponytail or chignon will do well with a delicate fascinator.

What Can a Fascinator Do For a Girl?

• A fascinator brings interest and attention to your face, highlighting your natural bone structure and eyes.

• A fascinator shows off your beautiful hair by adorning it with something special.

- A fascinator visually balances your shape or outfit with a nice little upward lifting of the eye.
- A fascinator is a most beguiling way to show off your personality and sartorial flair.

The summer holidays are just as fun but for some reason we don't seem to put as much effort into them. A Fourth of July barbeque is marred by a plastic tablecloth, every array of condiment in a sweaty plastic bottle, and stacks of paper dishes. Just because the living is easy doesn't mean it can't be pretty. Use a real tablecloth. If you don't have enough real plates and silverware, raid the thrift store, where flatware is 10 cents apiece and plates are a quarter, making it nearly cheaper than plasticware and certainly more environmentally friendly. Fill a cute metal ice tub with soapy water and have everyone throw their flatware in there to make clean-up a breeze. Another metal ice tub can be for dishes, so everyone knows where to leave their plates and glasses.

I love a home decked out in Americana for the summer. There's little more cheerful, especially in New England. Copious amounts of red geraniums and old-fashioned flag swags are about  as cheerful as a New England house can ask for. Just be sure you are hanging your flags correctly, and then go crazy.

Let me discuss parades for a moment. Oh, aren't they fun? I know it means traffic and wrangling the chairs and cooler and blankets and maybe the kids, but embrace it. Create the fanfare. Buy flags for waving from the kids selling them at the parade. Wear as much star-spangled jewelry and red-white-and-blue as you possibly can. I always do a Fourth of July manicure and pedicure, too. I've even been known to wear a rhinestone "USA" stick-on tattoo. And always,

always, always put your hand over your heart as a flag passes by. Yes, on the Fourth of July this may mean keeping your hand over your heart the entire parade. I adore that. Spirit is the stuff of life, and one of the best ways to capture memories.

A summer garden brunch is delightful and fun for any weekend, but especially for a birthday party. Real tablecloths again, of course, and tons of flowers. Just tons of flowers. On cakes, in little votive holders scattered down the table, in massive bunches on the buffet table, tucked in tall glasses placed inside wellies at the feet of the table . . . everywhere. Renting a tent is optional but it sure sets the scene. String lights, string bunting, stick pinwheels where the tent stakes are. Don't forget good old-fashioned lawn games. Croquet is perfect on the shady part of the lawn, and a giant outdoor Jenga set is entertainment for all ages.

If your summer event is an evening one, consider creating an outdoor movie. String up an ironed white sheet taut on a clothesline or from a porch or side of the house and project a movie onto it. Be sure to provide plenty of blankets, pillows, and chairs, as well as flashlights and citronella candles for a comfortable atmosphere. If you have a friend with a cotton candy, popcorn, or shave ice machine, now is the time to call in a favor and ask them to bring it over for the evening. Set up a fire pit if you've got the space (and a fire permit from your town if necessary) and have s'mores fixin's ready (don't forget the peanut butter cups).

When fall starts coming around it is time to get cozy and reconsider the "home arts." Apple picking is, of course, a tradition worth keeping. Make a list of your apple recipes ahead of time and add up the number of pounds you'll need so you don't end up throwing away gorgeous heirloom apples. Bring your red wagon, bring your camera, and bring your sense of adventure. But please be courteous . . . living in Vermont where there are precious heirloom apple orchards worth saving, I am conscious of their survival. Many people pick one apple of each kind, take one bite, and throw it on the ground. This is not only stealing from the orchard (not paying for the apples), but it is a waste for everyone. Try the samples in the barn if they're offering them, or set up your own tasting once you get home. You'll want apple cider donuts and warm apple cider, too, of course. And apple pie with a slice of sharp cheddar cheese on top, oh yes. That's a Vermont thing, but trust me, it's good. And carrot soup and baked potatoes and chili with peanut butter bread on the side, and oh the food of fall is so delicious I can't stand it.

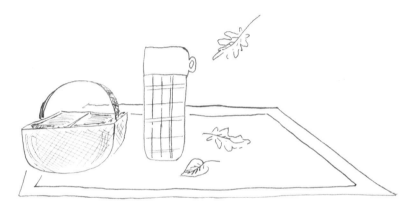

Fall is the beginning of plaid blanket and plaid thermos season. I love to collect these from thrift and antique stores. When you're looking for vintage plaid blankets, make sure they are in good shape with few to no holes if they're wool, no funky scents, no weird stains, etc. Hudson and Pendleton are the top brands to find. Wool blankets are a pain to wash, I admit, but it is a necessity for vintage blankets. Use the bathtub and wool wash, and hang them outside to dry. They'll capture that sweet, crisp fall air. When it comes to classic plaid thermoses, you can go the actual-vintage route if you're careful, or you can invest in the reproductions they have available now. Actual vintage ones tend to have rust, dents, and broken glass inside (shake them gently; if they make noise, they're broken and only good for decoration). Fall is my favorite season for canoeing as well, because the geese are migrating, the sun is intensely golden when it begins to set, and the air has a refreshing crispness that inspires one's paddling abilities. If you're a knitter, fall is your season. I love knitting, I really do, but everything I've ever made has come out totally unwearable. A hat that was supposed to fit me didn't even fit my friend's baby, and a poncho turned into a superhero cape . . . but that's neither here nor there. If you love to knit, please knit me a pair of socks and I will forever be in awe of you.

On Making Up Fun and Creativity

My grandpa would send me straight to a chair to literally twiddle my thumbs if I ever said I was bored. With our endless imaginations, how could we ever be bored? There is always poetry to be written, songs to be sung, cleaning to be accomplished, letters to be sent, ideas to be drawn, dances to be danced, gifts to be made, and the list goes on.

When I'm bored my first order of business is to find caffeine. Caffeine fixes boredom better than most anything else I know. Get a little caffeine crazy vibe going on and suddenly you're sanitizing wastebaskets and cleaning behind the fridge. Then it's on to finding music that suits my mood. I put my music on "random" and dance to whatever music comes on. This engages different parts of my brain, makes me laugh, and always entertains.

Reach Out

Once you're in a good groove, it's time to reach out to others. Boredom can easily turn into a pity party and that just won't do. This may mean texting a friend to go out for ice cream, or it may mean getting out all of your art supplies and painting cards for your faraway friends. Calling your grandma is always a good idea when you're bored. Bake muffins. Send postcards to kids in your life, I promise they will love it. Visit your neighbors (and bring them some of those muffins you baked). Actually doing something instead of giving in to another round of TV shows is the key to rising above boredom.

Invest in Your Future

When you're bored, it's the perfect time to try a new experience. We rarely regret trying new things, but we often regret not trying. I know you have something deep down that you want to turn into reality. A dream that follows your heart around like a shadow. Bring it into the light. I want to see what your heart carries with it, and I know others do, too. You want to start a bed & breakfast? Start writing that business plan. Want to become an EMT on the weekends? Sign up for a CPR class. Another great idea is to send yourself an email via "futureme.org." This website allows you to write yourself an inspiring, encouraging email and they deliver it to you a year in the future. I've done this for several years and I love it randomly popping into my email to remind me to keep investing in my future.

Get Your Creativity On

Get your creativity on. Creativity is like riding a bike, as they say. It always comes back to you, even when you've been out of practice for a while. If you're scared about getting out those watercolors, putting that pen to paper, or plucking those guitar strings again, simply begin at the beginning. Being a beginner is a marvelous thing. I love being a beginner. Beginners come to the table with enthusiasm, grit, and fresh perspective. They are eager; they eat up knowledge and seek new possibilities. Beginners see the beauty of the future. To be (or watch) a beginner is to be inspired again . . . to know that technique is foundational and rules are good but creativity is from the heart, and everyone has that.

Begin somewhere, anywhere. Start starting. Create, invent, make, do. Use your hidden moments to invest in your dreams. Boredom is no longer in your vocabulary, remember, or I might make you sit in a chair and twiddle your thumbs. Time is on your side if you use it well.

Another thing about creativity: it's an endless well. You can't use it up. In fact, it's self-feeding; the more you are creative, the more creativity you get. Of course, one can outpace the natural cycle and run out of inspiration if you're sprinting too fast. That happens to the best of us when we get over-committed. Nonetheless, begin filling the well again and it starts pouring forth double.

Photography

Take photos. Get a video camera. Capture moments. So many of my friends don't have the luxury of having home movies from when they were growing up. My family loves to get together and watch these, laughing until we are literally in pain. These are priceless memories. My brother has followed in our dad's foot-steps and purchased a video camera when my niece was born. Yes, I know we now have phones that can take videos, but they  are limited and I'm not sure how these will last into the future. In twenty years we'll all either have photos of every single meal we ever ate and millions of blurry videos or no tangible memories whatsoever. This whole "cloud" situation makes me nervous. I do not trust invisible storage.

Technology has definitely made the printing of photos easier, though. I entrust this to the professionals. You can have books made from your Instagram and sent to you monthly with no effort on your part, or you can design a keepsake book yourself, or simply print copies individually. Hard copies are the only safe copies of photos. I don't even trust the ink and photo paper of my home printer. Faded memories are . . . faded memories.

Growing up, my dad had a rule that we didn't take plain scenery photos on family vacations. Of course, artistic landscapes are different, but this was in the day of film photography when you paid for a roll of film twice—to purchase it and to develop it. His theory was that no one cares to look at landscapes in twenty years, but a family member in front of a landscape is a "keeper." Keepers are the "must-frame" ones, also known as "framers." So take keepers. Fill frames.

Speaking of keepers, in a different sense I am a keeper of things. I like to take documentary-style photos. Every so often I'll document my apartment, because I change it up frequently and want to see it through the years. I like pictures of cars I've had, me at jobs I've had and the like . . . documenting life so I have a record of people, places, and things I've known and loved. This is important to my poet's soul. My mom tells me she had a gold Camaro as her first car in the seventies and oh how I wish I had a photo of her in flares, Farah Fawcett hair, and this gold Camaro. I can picture her, rocked back on high wedge clogs, arms crossed, flashing a big smile, leaning on her car, proud as can be. I felt the same way about my first car, a boxy Honda Accord, but I'm not sure it has the same vintage panache.

Every few years I do a 365 photography project. This is a photo-a-day for a year, and it can be any photo or specifically a self-portrait. I've done both, but my years of self-portraits are beyond cherished memories to me. I can tell you exactly what I was doing and feeling every single day because I have a photo of it, and a photo of the outfit, the age, and the place. This project stretches your creativity and your photographic skill, and it will stretch your embarrassment levels. When you're halfway into the year and have a creative idea, you won't mind pretending to dig through the dumpster while others pass by, because you need to get the shot that's in your head. This is a very good exercise in self-confidence and creative confidence.

Celebrating Milestones:

The Arts of Celebration, Mail, and Care Packages

"I FEEL THERE IS NOTHING MORE ARTISTIC THAN LOVING PEOPLE." —VINCENT VAN GOGH

Life is tenuous and precious. I say that with certainty, having seen my fair share of the tough things in life, and maybe more than my fair share of some. And I say with even more certainty: this is why I celebrate the every day. Why I eat the cheesecake at midnight. Why I burn the nice candles instead of letting them gather dust. Why I send the good cards, with the true words, that I really mean. Because tomorrow? Tomorrow is not guaranteed. Nor is our next breath. I live life the way it is meant to be lived, with delight and surprise and wonder in my eyes. You might want to call me an escapist or a dreamer, and if I am those, then so be it. The world is sometimes worth escaping and it is always worth dreaming about a better future. I do not feel the need to build my life upon the rotten foundations of what can be reality. I will carry, instead, the banner of the good and beautiful and lovely.

There is so much to do in this life. Only, say, fifty more good birthdays, if we're lucky. A handful of Easters, really, and only a few dozen more Christmases. When I think of it that way I want to do the very best job I can of taking it all to heart, because that doesn't seem to be enough.

• • • • • • • • • • • • • •

The raspberries are plump
Sun-warmed and safe, here
And so are we these dappled days
Waiting and wanting for nothing

I roll dough with a light hand
Sprinkle sugar with abandon, everywhere I go
I say Yes, please and Yes, let's as often as possible
Go down to the river, take a picnic, take delight

I carry birthday candles and confetti in my bag
To celebrate the future or illuminate the shadows
You never know when you might need to call life
What it is, and people what they are: Magnificent
I like days like fluted pie crusts
Nights like a well-worn apron

I like my coffee sweet, my pillow soft
And my little home, happy and full.

● ● ● ● ● ● ● ● ● ● ● ● ● ●

I am not content living in the shadow of my past or hiding in my (potential) children's future. There is work for me to do, too. There is a mission statement in my life that goes above and beyond mundane tasks. That doesn't mean it is a big stage, or a famous name. In fact, I hope it isn't. That brings so much pressure and is such a demand on your time and life. No, no, I'm quite content to be behind-the-scenes orchestrating beautiful things to surprise and delight my nearest and dearest. Or strangers, they're good to surprise and delight too.

Have you heard of Hannah Brencher and her More Love Letters campaign? I've enjoyed participating in this movement for the past few years. Strangers write love letters (really, notes of encouragement and inspiration) that are left in public places for other strangers to happen upon. My favorite is to leave little love notes tucked in parking meters, on public bulletin boards, tucked in sugar bowls on café tables, under tips in that little black book at the end of a meal. The CEO of Aveda's original JUUT Salonspa hair salons, David Wagner, calls it being a Daymaker. His unique and touching story is of a client who came in one day outside of her regular appointment schedule,  and how their chat in the hairdressing chair changed her life. She wrote him later saying that she had come in to look good for her own funeral, as she was planning her suicide for that night. But the cheerful and inspirational interaction with David changed her mind. Her day was made. Her life was saved. That's what I'm talking about.

Sometimes we are the ones needing our day made. That's good, too. I love when a stranger buys me a coffee. What a lift to my day! I go around looking for ways to pay it forward. But I'm not a fan of those coffee-line chains where each car pays for the next car in line and it goes on indefinitely. I believe in small, random acts of kindness. Big ones are fine, too, but let's not make it nearly mandatory. I want it to be from the heart.

Embracing the idea that we can and should accept the gestures others offer into our lives is a big part of maturing in our inner selves. We are worthy of love. They say we only accept the love we think we are worthy of, and some of us reject it all. Be worthy deep down in your soul. Feel it.

I am a sharer, and I hope I never lose that. My mom used to call me her "show and tell girl" because I was always showing and telling her about every little detail of things. As an adult, I've translated that into a gift-giving mentality, combined with a terrible-at-keeping-secrets one. Which, depending on how you look at it, is a good or bad thing. I buy a gift in August for Christmas and cannot wait four months to give it to them. It burns a hole in my heart to not lavish that love on them *now*.

Sending Mail, a.k.a. "Mail Call Monday"

I've shared words from the time I was a tiniest tot, when I would make small books and set up a "shop" and sell them to my mom for a nickel. Business was brisk, not going to lie. My best friend and I (hi Lindsey!) made little vintage-style calling cards with our names by the dozens from the craft box under my bed filled with trims and stickers, embossers and pens of every color. I always loved the idea of a pen pal, and was a

letter-writer from then on. In college, I tucked notes in the school mail boxes of all of my friends, boys and girls alike. These days, I have pen pals from all over the country and world. We share postcards, specialty food, Christmas cards, and out-of-the-blue letters.

"Mail-Call Monday" is a take-off on the "mail call" at lunch during summer camp. It was always a bit terrifying, because if you got called for mail, you usually had to perform a ridiculous feat to get your letter, such as kiss a camp counselor on the cheek or do the chicken dance. But everyone loved getting mail anyway, because it was special and usually involved a few extra bucks for snacks at the canteen. I still love the idea of a "mail call" and most Mondays send off a pretty stack of letters, postcards, and packages (no funny antics required).

I live in a small town where I know my postmistress by first name (hi Holly!) and usually run into half a dozen people I know when checking my post office box. I know most people don't have this luxury in big city post offices, but I like those too. They're grimy and metallic and bustling. They're a hub, and a hub keeps the world going, keeps my mail trekking across the globe. I don't even mind lines. They're good for people-watching and funny conversations with strangers and deep thinking, and they're good for exercising your patience.

A stack of cards ready to go is just so pretty to me. Words, meant for you, winged across the wild winds. It's lovely, isn't it? I choose stamps for the seasons, personality, or color. Vintage stamps are particularly fun and I love to buy them from specialty dealers in person or online. My current favorites are Walt Disney 6-cent stamps, Grace Kelly 29-cent stamps and Mississippi 5-cent stamps. You have to actually lick them, and count to make sure you have the appropriate current postage rate. What a throwback!

Then there are the addresses, both return and recipient, where penmanship and color are the name of the game. I love big names, scroll-y names, giant and visible. Addresses are of slightly less importance, but I prefer them centered and stately. Hot pink pens are my favorite for white envelopes, and black envelopes are a chance to exercise my white pen, which does not hide flaws easily but is visually striking.

Illustrations, washi tape, and little quotes or notes on the back side are all fun additions. I am known for a little heart where the envelope flaps meet, at the very least. Sometimes I go all out, personalizing a scene for a friend or creating the same one on a handful of cards for an occasion. For Easter, I do a pretty calligraphy, "He is Risen!" and at Christmas, of course, a jolly "Merry Christmas!"

.These days stationery is easy to come by, but quality counts. I'm all about a thick, gorgeously luxurious cold-pressed note that feels regal to send and receive. Kate Spade's notecards fit this bill, as do Crane's and Smythson of Bond Street. A lesser-known favorite of mine is Felix Doolittle, whose stationery is adorned with watercolors of hedgehogs and cherry pies. These are expensive, to be sure, but the hand feel and quality makes them an utter pleasure to write and a keepsake for the recipient.

I wholeheartedly agree with Van Gogh that the way we love is our biggest and best artistic medium and pursuit. Which is why I'm all about loving on my people in big and small ways. Gift-giving and note-writing happen to come naturally to me, but I know that's not the case for everyone.

Good Gift-Giving

I'm a big fan of keeping my eyes out for gifts all year long. The hardest part for me is not giving them right away (and remembering where I put them). To combat that second one, I started keeping a special place for all gifts. A sturdy bag or box on a shelf in a closet will do just fine if you don't have a big trunk to hide things. You might have to get a bit more creative (or find a good lock!) if you have kids who rifle through everything.

The secret to good gift-giving is cleverness. But perhaps cleverness is not your strong suit. Here's a way to fake cleverness (I only claim this to work for gift-giving; off-label uses not covered) and to up your gift-giving game.

How to Fake Cleverness
1) Pay Attention
2) Theme it Up
3) Go Simple and Unique
4) Avoid the Big-Box Stores
5) If in Doubt, Go to the Grocery Store.

Pay Attention: This is what separates the amateurs from the professionals of gift-giving, and it's your first task in being clever. No need to go all Sherlock Holmes on it, just tuck away a few pieces of relevant information (Write. It. Down. Brains cannot be trusted to remember things!). Examples of relevant information: favorite color, sizes, coveted items, favorite scents, a trinket they had once and can't find again, favorite stores, anything "favorite" actually, etc. This allows for instant cleverness. Many times all you need to know is something they once had and can't find again. It sounds odd, but this actually comes up in conversation quite frequently. One time my dad was desperate for a specific kind of orange peeler. He couldn't find it anywhere. I tracked it down, all 99 cents of it, and it was one of the best-loved presents. Throw in a bag of oranges and you're golden. "How did you know?" will be the refrain as you pass out gifts.

Theme it Up: Using the above information, you can take things a step further to create an even cleverer gift. You've got their favorite color? Perfect. Theme it up, gift-basket-of-colored-items style. No one wants a basket of junk, though, so be judicious. Scarves, cookbooks, soaps, candles, food in color-aligned packaging, pens, a mug, a comfortable throw, decorative tin of tea, etc. are all perfect. The theme shouldn't be costume-y though; if someone collects cardinals, a cardinal-themed gift basket may be overwhelming to them. Instead, support the passion in other ways, such as birdseed and a book on how to attract birds to your backyard. Here's a gift idea that works for practically anybody: a movie-themed stack. Grab a $5 DVD from Target or Walmart, wrap it up. Grab 4 boxes of movie theatre candy from the dollar store and wrap each box individually. Top it off with a wrapped box of movie-theater-style popcorn, and tie the tower together with ribbon. Everyone loves a gift tower, candy, and a movie, and it's $10. Theme it up to their own tastes, and it's movie-themed, so double-theme-like-woah.

Simple and Unique: This is another way to go. If you're going simple, make sure it is unique, unique, unique. Soap can be a staid gift, but if it is unique it is stand-out. My mom is a coffee lover, and I found the jackpot of coffee-themed bath products handmade locally with coffee. You'd better believe I snapped those up! This goes hand-in-hand with the next tip.

Avoid the Big Box Stores: It is easy to swoop into Target and gather a handful of cute gifts. Trust me, I'm not above the Target haul. But big-box-store merchandise can be a potentially lifeless gift considering there are 150 others on the shelf behind each item. If you're doing a big-box-store run, go to the individual aisles where hobby items might reside. Try the travel aisle for a clever multi-national hair-dryer-clothing-steamer-grilled-cheese-maker for your niece backpacking through Europe next summer, or the camping aisle for a classic thermos for any man in your life.

If in Doubt, Go to the Grocery Store: There are all sorts of classic luxury food gifts you can pick up at the grocery store. These are things we often buy for other people but never splurge on for ourselves, so they are always a welcome treat. Go for chocolate-covered macadamia nuts and a macadamia-nut-flavored coffee, an assortment of indulgent chocolate bars, or a savory chef's mix of herbs and oils.

Small Gifts

Small gifts are perhaps my favorite gifts. I love to give little "I'm thinking of you" gifts and can't help myself. This can be easy to do for girlfriends (nail polish! cupcake liners! pink paper clips!) but harder for the men in our lives. For men it's best to go hobby-themed or basic, I've found. For hobby gifts, you may need to stroll down an aisle or go into a shop you don't usually frequent to pick up a little something-something for your man. New guitar picks, a new barbeque seasoning to try, a new fishing fly, fresh Moleskine notebook, etc. When it comes to basics, men always seem to need them, be it a pack of white tees or socks, dress socks, razor blades, or shaving cream, etc. I like to treat these as small gifts instead of necessities. "Hey I picked you up a new loofah for the shower because I know you don't like to be seen buying them," can be words of affection to a man's ears.

I buy small gifts for everyone. I found the most fabulous raspberry mohair vintage cardigan that I know will look darling on my illustrator (hi Emily!) and I can't wait another second to give it to her. It was all of $5 and a little bit of follow-through to actually buy it. How many times do we see little souvenirs that remind us of someone but we can't be bothered to follow through? I can be bothered. It isn't a bother, really, it's a pleasure. I'm such a gift-giver at heart. I truly adore it.

I buy coffee for co-workers I've known on a photography set for a day, bring in a giant bag of Reese's peanut butter cups by the second week because I know we'll need them to get through the last shot list. I find gifts everywhere . . . have found the most lovely river stones with encouragement engraved on them for $1.99 at the gas station checkout for a dear friend's mom during a difficult time. Found vintage linen-paper postcards of my town at a random souvenir-shop to send a friend who collects vintage ephemera. There need be no occasion. Life, and enjoying doing life with someone, whether it be on a two-day photography shoot or a friend of decades, is reason enough.

Wrapping and Presentation

I tend to be like a five-year-old, shoving the gift into the recipient's hands while shouting, high-pitched, "Open it, open it, open it!" Wrapping, though, I do love. Each year at Christmas I choose a theme and enjoy looking at the pile of pretty presents under my tree for a few weeks before they get sent off to their various around-the-country new homes. But gift-giving in general can be stressful. Here are a few tips.

First things first: Never be embarrassed about giving a gift. It seems we get shy because giving a gift can expose us to scrutiny. Nope. We've spent time and effort (and perhaps money) on a gift, which should never open one up to scrutiny. Shore yourself up and remember, the gift is an offering of your love, not an invitation to a comment on your self-worth.

Secondly: Have fun! The best way to make wrapping enjoyable is to be prepared. Pick up cute giftwrap and gift bags as you see them, even if you don't know exactly what you'll use them for. Stockpile ribbons, doo-dads to attach to packages, and tissue paper. For some reason the one thing I usually run out of is tissue paper for gift bags, so I always snap up good colors or plain white when I see it.

I've used plain kraft paper, custom-made photo wrapping paper, vintage wrapping paper, dollar store wrapping paper, newspaper, super-thick and expensive one-sheet wrapping paper, and more. For a baking themed gift, wrap it in a few layers of parchment paper and secure it with baker's twine. For children, wrap gifts in coloring book pages.

Embrace imperfection: I like to keep some packages oddly-shaped and twisted at the ends or fluffed at the top and tied with ribbon. It keeps things interesting and imperfect, especially if piled amongst a bunch of lovely wrapped rectangles. Use creative containers. One year when I was a kid, my mom sewed together a bunch of new socks for me end to end and tucked it inside a paper towel tube she wrapped like candy. When I pulled out one sock, it kept coming like a magician's scarf. And one of the best gifts I have ever received was wrapped in a paper grocery bag, but inside it was filled with thought and intention.

Swedish tradition: A Scandinavian tradition that I love is to create a little riddle or rhyme to top each package. The riddle relates to what is inside, of course, while aiming to trick the recipient. This is fun for everyone!

The Art of the Care Package or the "Just Because" Box

I simply love a good "just because" box. I think the words "just because" are some of the sweetest that can be said. They say so much while saying . . . well, nothing. They say, "I care, I'm thinking about you, I love you, I want to be present in your life even when you are far away, I know you, I didn't forget you" and so much more. Just because boxes are random and that's the fun of it, but here are a few ideas on what to include.

Something Edible: What says, "I know you and I love you," more than their favorite snack food? This is universal. This is particularly exciting if it is a regional snack that they can't get away from home. I'm talking Georgia boiled peanuts or Pearson's Peppermint Patties from St. Paul.

Something Useful: Just a little trifle to make life easier, such as a new lip balm or post-it notes. Everyone loves to be taken care of and "Mom-ed" a bit with something new and useful.

Something Adorable: This is anything that elicits an *awwww*: anything miniature, fuzzy, featuring cute puppies, or that brings up a memory.

Something Luxurious: A little extra that they wouldn't buy for themselves, such as a gift card for a fancy coffee drink, new mittens, or any little thing that made you think of them.

The real clincher for a "just because box" is a funny and random item. A conversation piece when it is sitting on the kitchen counter, dorm room desk, or office desk. A raucous laugh to counter the "aww" factor. When my brother was in college this was the Staples "Easy" button. He and his dorm-mates had them everywhere. Taped on ceilings so they could jump and hit them. Under desks for a surprise "easy" attack. I've seen bacon gum, cupcake-flavored floss, Dali-melting-clock Band-Aids, and all sorts of little things that will be a perfect silly "just-because."

Care packages needn't be giant boxes that are expensive to send. Using this formula, you can make a care package that fits in a first-class padded envelope easily. For a friend going through a rough patch, pick up a chocolate bar or two, a new lip balm, a card with kittens, a gift card for a coffee, and a magnet with a funny saying. Or go all out and do send a giant box that is expensive to ship, because life is short. Load it up with junk food for your favorite college student, maybe throw some laundry detergent in there as a subtle hint, make their favorite cookies and include those for the "Awww" factor, throw in a little cash for the "luxuries" only a college student can desire (pizza at midnight?). Then of course, you'll need to work a bit harder on the funny/random element for a college student, but you can do it. Inside jokes are a great way to get inspiration. My brother and I love to quote a movie line from *Napoleon Dynamite*, "How we feelin' 'bout this here 32-piece-set?" Go find a 32-piece set of *anything* so long as it has those words on the box and sticky a note on it that says, "How we feelin' 'bout this here 32-piece-set?" Best gift ever.

Using the Good China

I know, I know. The good china has to be handwashed. But do it. The good china might break. Use it anyway. It's worth it. The good china sets the day apart and seeps into memories. The gold edge of a plate makes the heart flutter a bit more than the standard dinner plate. The good china is to be used to celebrate the good life, and dang it, your life *is* good and *is* worth celebrating. As-is. Right now.

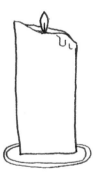

The same goes for the luscious candles, the special napkins, the delicate glassware . . . they are designed to enhance your life. They are made to be used. The best part is, when the good candle is used up, you get to buy another one, or you have room on your shelf for a gift that might come your way. There will always be more fancy things. If a cup chips, no worries. It has been used and broken with love. I think that's better than intact and unused.

Anything kept too long gets stale, collects dust, becomes forgotten. Our eyes become accustomed to it, our senses lose the feeling of luxury. Use that gorgeous stationery, that delicious olive oil, that saffron a friend brought back from a trip. Be liberal with the bath salts from the Dead Sea, slather on the lotion with that gorgeous Givenchy scent. Soak it up, savor it.

The trick is to enjoy and savor the fancy things as you use them. If you have children, it is fun to teach them the importance of special things and being "fancy" with them. They love being able to use fancy and important grown-up things and they'll rise to the occasion with straight backs, two hands on the glasses, and being extra careful. I know accidents still happen. Assure them that even if something is broken, they did an excellent job of being fancy and it was just an accident. Truly, it happens to the best and most "grown-up" of us.

Creating Traditions

Oh creating traditions is one of my favorite things. Traditions are such a deep part of the history we carry within us, so I make as many as I can. Creating traditions is basically creating memories, and I'm a memory-maker.

Any little quip or bit that becomes a "thing" between you and someone else, or even just in your own life, is a tradition. Traditions needn't be stuffy, big things, such as a full-on turkey dinner at Grandma's house *every year just because*. Traditions change, shift, and can be small or large. In fact, I prefer small traditions to big ones because they are easier to pull off and don't require as much effort. Effort is good, to be sure, but so is low-effort these days. Let's create sustainable traditions for a new generation.

Many of my traditions are birthday-related, which seems like a good place to start since my birthday is at the beginning of the year. Every year I plan my birthday outfit with the sole aim of looking like a "confection"—a cream puff, a frothy pink milkshake, with layers of tulle and cashmere and fur, and of course my big mink earmuffs because it's January. Underneath it, though, I'll wear my special birthday lingerie. This, too, is usually pink, frothy, silky, or frilly (or all of the above!), and chosen specifically with a celebration in mind. Choosing birthday lingerie has become a special tradition for me, and I've ended up with a delightfully happy lingerie drawer because of it. I also choose a birthday song each year, one that I replay all day and that seems to fit the mood of the day and year.

Another winter tradition is what I call "shower candles." These are candles that I light in the bathroom while I'm taking a bath or shower and I usually get a scent like "Warm Laundry" or "Clothesline in Spring" that feels fresh-fresh-fresh. I love the company of a candle for an evening or morning shower. On winter mornings, it is often dark and cold, so I'll turn on the heater and light the candle. For evening showers in winter, I cozy-it-up big time. I love a clear shower curtain liner for the sole purpose of enjoying the warm glow of the candle. It feels sensual and spa-like to shower by candle light, even if you only have five minutes.

One tradition that is new to my repertoire is to leave friends oranges wrapped in cheerful cloth on their doors in the dead of winter. Citrus is in season, and what a delightful little piece of Florida sunshine. Try to find Cara Cara oranges if you can; they're a cross between a sweet pink grapefruit and an orange and are utterly delicious. Use pinking shears to cut squares or circles of cheerful (preferably yellow!) fabrics big enough to wrap up an orange and leave a nice frill at the top. Then attach a ribbon around to tie it and create a handle to hang on a door. I like to make little watercolor cards, too, with a little saying like, "Spring is coming!" or "A bit of sunshine for you!" These small indulgences are sure to put smiles on faces and they look immensely happy in a basket as you go around surprising your friends.

I have friends who go all out on February 2, Groundhog Day, when Punxsutawney Phil tells us good news about an early spring or breaks our hearts with six more weeks of winter. They make groundhog-shaped meatloaves, play "toss the hog," and celebrate the shifting light that accompanies the beginning of February, regardless of whether or not Phil sees his shadow.

Some friends have decided that whenever they get together, someone has to bring a bacon-flavored food item. This has resulted in epic wins and epic culinary disasters, as well as plenty of memories. Other friends have a little string of lantern-shaped lights in their kitchen and every time I come over, I turn them on, much to their fake chagrin. They chide me but laugh every time they see them and say, "Oh, Natalie was here!" I periodically leave them packs of batteries for the lights to continue the joke.

Traditions expand our days and give us a little something to look forward to. Traditions celebrate life, celebrate people, and celebrate happiness. What more could a girl want?

About the Author

Hi friends!

Natalie here, a modern lifestyle philosopher who is all about happy things for happy people. "Happy, Pretty, Messy" is my life motto and one I infuse into my daily life and all of my creative work. I keep my creativity busy, too, through poetry, writing books, food styling, giving gifts, sending mail, baking pies, and more. I run a creative studio in Brattleboro, Vermont above a flower shop that my best friend's parents have owned for forty years. There's also a pink-and-white-striped awning next door, home to a darling little ice cream shop I frequent all too often.

I wrote *Happy Pretty Messy* to share this philosophy with you: we can find beauty in the everyday things, strength in the toil, and deep wells of bravery in our souls. Life doles out blows to the best of us, some big and bruising, others small and simmering. And happy, pretty, messy is found through all of it, in all of it, and in all of us. I truly believe it changes lives. And I sure hope this book changes yours, at least in some small way, for the happier. You deserve to be beautiful and brave. I'm cheering you on.

I have a Master's degree in Poetry from Dartmouth College and my work has been featured in *The New Yorker*, *Life: Beautiful*, *Darling Magazine*, *Wilderness Magazine*, and more.

You can find my first book, *Gifts in Jars*, also by Skyhorse Publishing, my #caffeinecrazy mugs, and more ways to follow along with my happy, pretty, messy adventures by visiting www.nataliewise.com. Let's be friends!